Coastal Archaeology of Western India
With Special Reference to Goa

M. Nambirajan

2007
Kaveri Books
New Delhi - 110 002

First Published in 2007

ISBN 81-7479-079-9

Published by
Rakesh Goel
Kaveri Books
4697/5-21 A, Ansari Road,
New Delhi - 110 002 (India).

Tel.: 011-2328 8140, 2324 5799
e-mail: kaveribooks@vsnl.com

Laser Typesetting by
Aarati Computers, Delhi - 110 009.

Printed at
Chawla Offset Printers, Delhi-52.

PRINTED IN INDIA

FOREWORD

Early 1960s is an important period in the History of archaeological researches in Goa region. In 1964, the Archaeological Survey of India undertook large-scale conservation and restoration work to the magnificent monuments i.e. the churches of the early Portuguese period in old Goa. At the same time a programme of village-to-village survey of archaeological and historical remains in the region, was initiated. Later, a regular and permanent office of the Archaeological Survey of India, namely Goa Mini Circle, was established. An Archaeological Museum was reorganized on scientific lines. The Circle office since then is systematically carrying out both, conservation of all the monuments, declared protected by the Survey, and exploration of archaeological remains. There is also a Dept. of Archives, Archaeology and Museums, Government of Goa. In early 1990s at the dynamic initiative of Dr. S.R.Rao, a retired Superintending Archaeologist of the Survey, a Marine Archaeology Wing was established in the National Institute of Oceanography, Dona Paula, Goa. The Under Water Archaeology work along the Indian coasts that is being carried out by the Wing is known all over the world. Thus, by and by, an academic atmosphere for archaeological research was built up encouraging higher research and study in Archaeology. Being, therefore, inspired by the prevailing academic condition, an young, energetic and enthusiastic Officer of the Survey, Sri (later Dr.) M. Nambirajan, the author of this book, came forward with a proposal of carrying out Ph.D. research on Archaeology of Goa to me when I was a Professor in the Dept. of Studies in Ancient Indian History and Epigraphy, Karnatak University, Dharwad.

Prior to 1960s, with the exception of the Kerala belt, replete with hundreds of Iron Age megalithic burial sites, many with sepulchral monuments typical of the area such as *Kudaikal, Topikal,* rock-excavated chamber, besides Stone circle with or without cairn packing, port-hole chamber, menhir, as well as Rock engravings in Edakkal caves, are discovered since 1823, the entire coastal region from south of Mumbai to Tiruvananthapuram, was hardly known for Pre and Protohistoric cultural heritage. Even the immediately succeeding early historical stage of the human settlements in the region, was almost virtually blank. The lonely reference to '*Keralaputa*' and, '*Satiyaputa*' in the Major Asokan edicts II and IV, the latter being doubtfully identified with Dakshin Kanada district (bifurcated recently into two districts: Mangalore and Udupi) by some scholars till recently and a few stray references to places and coastal ports of commercial importance in anonymous writer's Periplus of Erithrean Sea of c. 1st century B.C. and Ptolemy's "A Guide to Geography", Roman coins found in one or two places such as Eyyal, etc., constituted the basic materials for restoring, vaguely, one or two aspects of the earliest part of the history of the region. In fact, the region was culturally considered to be a land of isolation, in view of the north-south oriented mighty Sahyadri (Western) ghats all along not easily surmountable; thick wild evergreen forests and heavy rainfall in the coastal-ghat and the adjacent Malnad region. As well as apparently non-availability of rock materials suitable for preparing stone tools. Even Proto-historic communities, let alone the Palaeolithic peoples, were supposed to be not appropriately equipped with tools and weapons to meet the environmental challenges for making inroads into the region.

The above supposition looked true in consideration of important notices of the monuments, sculptures, and inscriptions etc. all of the historical periods in the course of an earnest field survey by Fr.S.J. Heras during early 1930s. Of these, the most noteworthy are the rock-excavated Saiva caves with Siva-lingas of 3rd-5th century, i. e. of early Kadamba. The earliest cultural relic is a seated Buddha image of c. 2nd century in Colvale.

The chance discovery of the butt end of a ground stone axe and a fluted core, evidently of the Neolithic culture in the Chalcolithic stage by me in April 1964, that was immediately followed by the discovery of numerous Mesolithic sites mostly with quartz tools, in some parts of Goa and one or two stray ground stone axes in the upper reaches of the Mandovi river, during the regular village-to-village survey of archaeological and historical relics by S. A. Sali, of the Archaeological Survey of India, was a turning point in the matter of research in the Prehistory of the land. In the coastal region outside Goa, mostly in 1970s-80s, notices of neolithic axes were in a few places such as Mantrothurut (Quilon dist.), Koduvalli (Kozikodu dist.), Kathiroor (Cannanore dist.); neolithic burnished grey ware bowls with post firing red ochre paintings along the edge in Chitrari area (Wynad dist.), all in Kerala; further north of Kerala, neolithic ground axes with sharp polished working edge form in four places, namely, Bandimatha, Haradi, Kotatattu etc. in the Sita valley; rock cut chambers found in Bommarabettu near Udupi and subsequently in many other places and port - hole chambers Bada Kajekaru, Beluru, Kakkunje; and in the Malnad region adjacent to the ghat, many neolithic sites in thick forest area receiving the heaviest rainfall as at Nilaskal, Yadegudde near Tirthahalli etc. on the one hand and Early and Middle Palaeolithic sites in the Netravati valley near Mangalore and also in Kerala as numerous Mesolithic sites in different areas of the central zone of the coastal land, have substantially revealed the immense potentiality of the entire coastal region awaiting positive investigations into the

Prehistoric cultures, and at the same time setting aside all the previous suppositions regarding the environmental conditions being exceedingly difficult for the Protohistoric communities poorly equipped to meet the challenges for settling down in the region.

Statira Guzder is perhaps the first to investigate the Stone Age cultures of the coastal land of Maharashtra through field explorations. Her scientific work is "Quaternary Environment and Stone Age Cultures of Coastal Maharashtra" (1980). A little later follows Rajendran's investigation into the Early and Middle palaeolithic sites and also many Mesolithic sites in Karnataka and Kerala. His book "Prehistoric Cultures and Environment" (1989) is based on the materials from the explorations and a small-scale excavation of a Mesolithic site in Tenmalai.

Keeping in view of all the discoveries and studies up to late 1980s, Nambirajan with confidence decided to concentrate on the Pre-and proto-historic cultural stages of Goa region located between Kerala-Karnataka and Maharashtra; systematically carried out explorations in the untapped 120 localities out of 250 in the region, bringing to light many more new sites including an important Middle Palaeolithic site in Anakhane; carefully collected the materials and conducted methodical probing in the cave site at that revealed a continuous occupation from the Early Palaeolithic to Mesolithic through Middle-Upper Palaeolithic; worked out the statistical analysis site-wise and tool-type wise; recognized the areas of concentrations, of less and least settlement patterns; tried to understand the behavior of the moving communities and their settlements in relation to the rise and fall in Sea-level and of the tidal rivers flooding large tracts of the adjacent lands and the areas of the availability of rock and other materials on the one hand and by using the data obtained by multi-disciplinary applications by other scientific experts such as R.V. Joshi, Rajguru, Brockner Helmut, and others, on the other. The notable capacity of the Prehistoric communities to adapt their life style to different environmental situations, be it coastal land or the hilly down-ghat zone, could be appreciated. The result is the emergence of a broad out-line of the continuous Prehistoric and Protohistoric cultural development through the ages. Nay, distinguishing from the other similar valuable studies relating to the region by Goudellar who along with Kori Settar discovered the first Acheulian bi-facial tools in the region and others mentioned above, he has tried to carry through the archaeological narration into the Early historical period up to the stage from where the further story of the ancient peoples, could reliably be better reconstructed with rich archaeological and inscriptional and literary data. Augmented with appropriate data, tables, illustrations and their scientific studies, the narration is dispassionate, lucid and cogent.

It is also true that the picture of the Pre and Proto-historic people presented herein is very, very fragmentary with numerous large gaps. The Iron Age Megalithic culture and the Rock art need to be investigated on a large scale. The Neolithic cultural stage is equally another area where a thorough investigation is necessary. But the well-documented present study based on comprehensive field survey and with the limited, relevant scientific data from the areas, is what at best it could be at this stage that provides an encouraging, dependable base for future investigators for planning more thorough investigations involving scientific disciplines and methods. We hope he or some one else competent and well trained for the strenuous study will pick up the thread and continue the work more fruitfully. The present author therefore richly deserves to be congratulated for this good piece of work and our gratitude too.

Prof. A. Sundara

Soundaryashree, Bharati Nagara,
Dharwar, Karnataka.

ACKNOWLEGEMENT

I am extremely beholden to my Guru & Guide Prof. A. Sundara, for teaching me the fundamentals of research. Learning from him has been a great experience. My gratitude to him and his wife, who always played the perfect hostess, cannot be expressed in a few words. He also kindly agreed to write the foreword to this work.

I am greatly indebted to the authorities of Karnataka University, Dharwar, for all the encouragement during the course of my research.

Many a great soul in the Archaeological Survey of India helped me in my work. I am grateful to Shri D.K.Sinha, Superintending Archaeologist (Retd), Archaeological Survey of India, for giving necessary official permission to carry out the research; Shri K.V.Rao, Deputy Superintending Archaeologist (Retd.), Shri K.K. Muhammed, Superintending Archaeologist, Dr. S.K.Joshi, Shri R.S.Kulkarni, Asst. Superintending Archaeologist (Retd.) and Shri Gangadhar Korgaonkar, Sr. Conservation Assistant, for all the support and encouragement; Dr. T. Sundarajan, Assistant Superintending Archaeologist, for critical analysis of the work; Shri G.Thirumoorthy, Assistant Archaeologist, Shri P.V.Rajan, Librarian, Shri H. Raghavendra, Draughtsman, and Shri R. Jeyaraj, Photographer,

Archaeological Survey of India for helping in various ways in my work; Shri Devidas Bhomkar, Parshuram Kadam, Prakash Mahale and Damodar Fatde for accompanying me during field trip.

My sincere thanks are due to the Director and staff of the Dept. of Archives, Archaeology and Museums, Govt. of Goa, especially to Dr. Shirodkar, Director (Retd.), (Late) Mitragotri, Asst. Superintending Archaeologist, Shri Deshpande, Asst. Suptdg. Archaeologist, Shri A. Yalgi and Shri R. Sambrekar, librarians, Shri R. Naik, and Nayan Naik.

(Late) Dr.Rahunath Bhatt, Director Kannada Studies, Karnataka University, Prof. Shanta Kumari (Retd.), Dr.V.S.Padigar, Prof. and Chairman, Dept of History and Epigraphy, Karnataka University, Dharwar provided valuable guidance and advice. I am grateful to them.

I am immensely indebted to Dr. A.S. Gaur, Dr. Sila Tripati, Dr. Sundaresh, National Institute of Oceanography, Goa, for all the help rendered during the fieldwork.

I am extremely thankful to Shri Shaji Mohan for preparing the pencil drawing of the stone tools; Smt. Rema Naik and Smt. Latha Prashanth for neatly typing the manuscript.

My mother Neelamani, Smt.Kala my wife and my children Karthik, Akshath and Ankith, for all the support and cooperation in completing my research.

Shri Rakesh Goel, Kaveri Books, New Delhi, for bringing out the book in record time.

Last but not the least, my thanks are due to the Almighty without whose blessing & this work would not have been completed.

— M. Nambirajan

Contents

List of Plates

1

INTRODUCTION

Goa is located in middle of the west coast of India within the latitudes of 14° 53' 27" N and 15° 27' 29" N and longitudes of 73° 40' 54" E and 74° 20' 11" E. Ratnagiri and Sawantwadi districts of Maharashtra on the North, Belgaum and Dharwad districts of Karnataka on the East and Uttara Kannada district on the south form the boundaries of Goa. On the west the Arabian Sea forms the boundary. The Goa State extends about 60 kms East- West and 105 kms North- South and covers an area of about 3610 Sq.kms.

Perched on the western slopes of the Sahyadri Mountains, Goa is known for its scenic beauty with swaying coconut groves, red soil, lush green high lands, and silver sand beaches. Variously called the Golden Goa, the Rome of the East, etc., it attracted the attention of foreign travellers, Arab merchants, Indian and European rulers alike.

In the Gudea records datable to 2143 B.C. in the city-state of Lagash there is a mention of a place called Gubi. Dhume (1985:118) identified Gubi with Goa and suggested Gubi as the source word of Goa. The scholar, making an attempt to trace the etymology, does not give strong evidences to support his hypothesis. Further, it is not yet known whether Goa was so important around 2100 B.C. to find a place in the Lagash records. On the other hand, the term Gubi can be rendered to Goa as well as Gobi, the name of a desert in Mangolia. It is not yet known whether there was any contact between Lagash and Gobi region when the latter perhaps was not a desert. It may be noted that there were contacts between Sindhu valley and Lagash during that period especially in terms of trade and commerce. Therefore, it is more probable that Gubi is Goa, which had contact with Sindhu valley. If this surmise is correct, then this is the earliest reference to the Goa region.

Some scholars (Dhume, 1985:206) have unconvincingly tried to trace the origin of the word Goa to *Goem – Bab*, a mundari word, meaning an inclined ear of paddy and *guwi*, the Assamese term for areca nut. It is also suggested that Goa is derived from rishi Gautama who is supposed to have lived here (Satoskar 1982:28-31). Some scholars feel that Gomati, the ancient name of the river Mandovi, is the source of the word. Goa was one of the *sakthapitas* and *Gomati* was a presiding deity (Sirkar 1973; 27,67 & 85). Couto traced the origin of the word to *Goemot* (fertile and refreshing land) while D'Souza traced it to Goubat a local deity. Paes suggested that Guahalladeva, a Kadamba king of the tenth century A.D., has the probable origin of the word. However, the name of Goa appears to be well known even before, the advent of, Kadambas as known from the Mahabharata and the Puranas. Goa is referred to as Goparashtra and Goarashtra in the above works (Kamat 1990:5). Therefore, it is incorrect to say that the name is derived from the name of Guhalladeva, the Kadamba king.

The name by which Goa was known to the Greeks is still a matter of dispute. It is variously identified with Nelkinda and Aegedii of Periplus (Schoff 1974; 202). It is also identified with Cherosonesus and Kouba of

Ptolemy (Mc Crindle 1885; 180-1) and Nelkanydone of Plini (Fonseca 1986:117). The Arab name for Goa is also shrouded in mystery. It is generally identified with Kuve or Kuwa (Fonseca 1986:118). Ibn Batuta mentioned Sandabur, which is identified with Goa (Danes 1989: 170-81). On the other hand, Siddi Ali, a Turkish Admiral, identified Goa with Gowai Sandabur (Yule & Burnell 903:379).

After considering the various probabilities, only a few of them appear to be valid. A region may be named after the name of a river or the distinct characteristic features of a land. Hence, the derivation of the word Goa from *Gomati* or *Goemot* appears to be logical and of great antiquity.

Goa, *Goem* in Konkani language, was probably the Gomantaka, Govarashtra, Gomanchala and Goparashtra of Mahabharata and the Puranas. Since *Go* means cow in Sanskrit, Goarashtra refers to a land of cows. In the Harivamsapurana (Ch. 96-99), Goa is referred to as Gomanchala and as the scene of a battle between lord Krishna and Jarasandha. It is also believed that Lord Krishna, enchanted by the beauty of the land and the *gopikas,* named it Goparashtra. *Shurparka desa* is another name by which Goa was known (Kamat 1990:5). *Sahyadri khanda* of Skanda purana refers to the reclamation of a part of Goa from the sea by Parasurama, the sixth incarnation of Vishnu (Shastri, 1971). According to the traditions Goa is called *Parasurama kshetra*. However, the traditions prevailing in coastal Karnataka do not include Goa in the *Parasurama kshetra*. But the traditions existing in Maharashtra include Goa in the *Parasurama kshetra*. Thus, the extent of *Parasurama kshetra* varies from region to region. These traditions will be discussed in the chapter on Early Historical Period.

The Shiroda copper plate of Devraja of Bhoja dynasty (E.I., xxiv, 1984; 133-45) refers to Chandraur or Chandrapura (modern Chandor) as his capital. It has been identified with Sandabur of Arab records. The 5th century A.D. copper plates of Chandravarman of Konkan Maurya dynasty refer to Shivapura, the modern Shiroda. Bandora copper plates of Amarjitavarman (610 A.D.) of the same dynasty refer to Kumardvipa, modern Kumbharjuva. A Chalukyan inscription datable to 610 A.D. refers to Goa as Konkan Vishaya. In the inscription of Rattaraja of southern Silaharas dynasty, Goa is referred to as Simhaladvipa (Mirashi; 1977; ii).

The inscription of Chattya Deva II (1005-50) calls the island of Goa as Lamka (JBBRAS, Vol.9; 266) and the king is called Abhinava Lamkapura vara. Another Kadamba inscription dated to 12th century A.D. refers to Gopaka. Vijayanagara inscriptions refer to Goa as Gove, while Adilshahi inscriptions call it Guve (ARIE; 1962-63).

The archaeological and numismatic evidences point to Satavahana rule over Goa, before the Bhojas established their stronghold. Excavations carried out at the temple site at the Kota in Chandor yielded Satavahana copper coins and medieval potsherds and bricks of an earlier temple under the existing one. But so far no Satvahana inscription has been reported from Goa. The earliest available inscription is the Shiroda copper plate of Devaraja of Bhoja dynasty datable to 4th century A.D. The grant mentions that Devaraja was ruling from Chandrapura and probably his kingdom included Sashti (Salcette) Kuthahalli (Cortallim), Antruz (Ponda), Baradesh (Bardez), Ela (Old Goa) and part of Karnataka. Two more copper plates of the Bhojas were found from Bandora (Ponda) Goa. Asokan edicts mention the Bhojas as ruling over Konkan and Vidharbha. However, the relationship between the two is not yet clearly known. The copper plates do not mention the genealogy of the Bhojas.

The Konkan Mauryas, probably a branch of the Mauryas of Pataliputra, replaced the Bhojas under the suzerainty of Mahishmati in the early 5th century A.D. Two copper plates of this dynasty are known so far. They are, the Shivapur a grant of Chandravarman, datable to c. 5th A.D. recording the donations offered to the Buddhist *Mahavihara* at Shivapura, the modern Shiroda (Sanguem Taluk) and the Bandora copper plates of Amirjitavarman datable to c. 6th century A.D.

Under the Chalukyas of Badami, Goa, was probably formed part of *irridige vishaya* governed by one Swamikaraja. Later, Satyasraya and Dhruvaraya Indravarman of Batpur family and Vijayaditya ruled this region. Thereafter, the queen of Chandraditya, after the death of her husband, administered the affairs of irridige vishaya on behalf of her minor son. The Badami Chalukyas ruled over Goa until 750 A.D.

In around 765 A.D. Goa passed on to southern Silaharas with the capital at Gopakapattana, under the overlordship of the Rashtrakutas. The Kharepattana and Balipattana plates of southern Silaharas mention the genealogy of the Rashtrakutas as well as the genealogy of the Silaharas. Valipattana, a fortified city mentioned in their plates, has variously been identified with Valavli in Sawantwadi, Kharepattana near Vijayadurg, both in Maharashtra, Balli and Veli in Goa (Gazetteer of Goa: 1979:85). Tiswadi was probably under their control as there are references to Simhaladvipa in the Kharepattana grant of Rattaraja dated to 1008 A.D., (Mirashi: 1977; 107). Jayasimha Chalukya defeated Rattaraja in around 1020 A.D. when he rebelled against him. As the Chalukyas did not consolidate their victory the northern Silaharas usurped the Konkan region.

However, the southern Silaharas regained control and ruled over Goa till they were overthrown by the Goa Kadambas.

The Goa Kadambas ruled over the Konkan region from the middle of 12th century A.D. to the latter part of 14th century A.D. Their family deity was Saptakoteswara. They held lion as their lanchana. Chattaya or Shastadeva I was the founder of the dynasty with the capital at Chandrapura. The southern Silaharas continued to exercise control over some parts of Goa with the headquarters at Gopakapattana till Shastadeva II defeated them and took Gopakapattana, Ela and the Konkan in 900 A.D. His successor Jayakesi I (1050-1080 A.D.) also known as Viravarman declared himself as the lord of Konkanrashtra and shifted his capital from Chandrapura to Gopakapattana, which developed into a great commercial centre. Though the Kadambas under Guhalladeva II (1080-1100 A.D.) lost Kapardikadvipa and Irridige Vishaya to Northern Silaharas, Jayakesi II (1104-1148 A.D.) recovered them and declared himself independent of western Chalukyas. However, he was defeated and forced to accept the overlordship of western Chalukyas.

During the reign of Vishnuchitta (1148-87 A.D.) Goa Kadambas suffered defeats at the hands of the Kadambas of Hangal and Hoysalas. Although Jayakesi III (1187-1286 A.D.) and Tribhuvana Malla (1216-38 A.D.) tried to restore the glory, the Goa Kadambas were reduced to the position of local chieftains. Malik Kafur, the General of Allauddin Khilji, who plundered and destroyed Gopakapattana in the early 14th century A.D., forced them to shift the capital to Chandrapura, which increased their agony. In 1327 A.D., Chandrapura was razed to the ground by Muhammed-bin-Tuglaq resulting in the transfer of capital back to Gopakapattana. They were subjected to further attack by Nawab Jamal-uddin of Honawar. However, Goa did not pass on either to the Delhi Sultans or Bahmanis as the intention of attack was only plundering or looting. This is indicated in the Koragaon copper plates of 1351 A.D., which mentions one Bhima Bhopal ruling over Tiswadi, Bardez and Pernem from Gopakapuri (Gune 1977:49). He was probably a feudatory under the Kadambas but usurped power taking advantage of their decline.

Realising the importance of the Port of Goa, both the kings of Vijayanagara dynasty and Bahmani Sultans aspired to establish their domination over it resulting in frequent shifting of control over Goa from 1536 A.D. onwards. From 1390 to 1472 A.D. Goa was under the control of Vijayanagara forming part of Aragutti rajya with the capital at Govapuri. In 1472 A.D., the Bahmanis took over Goa and merged it with Junnar province. When the Bahmani kingdom broke into five Gosas the Goa region came under the Adilshahis of Bijapur (1489-1686 A.D.). As Gopakapattana lost its commercial importance due to the silting of river Zuari, Adilshahis developed Ela (Old Goa) as an alternative Port. Goa yielded 4 lakh Pardous a year from customs duty on everything that entered the port. Their desire to own such a lucrative port located strategically, spurred the Portuguese to attack Goa in 1510 A.D.

Practically, the whole of Goa is covered by the rocks of Dharwar super group of Archaean Proterozoic age except a strip in the north eastern part of the state which is covered by the Deccan trap of the upper Cretaceous – lower Eocene age. Roughly the upper group is called the Goa group. It constitutes a eugeosynclinal assemblage of rocks and is divided into four formations in the order of superimposition namely, Barcem formations which include 1. Metavolcanic rocks with minor Meta sedimentary. 2. Sanvordem formations include metagrey whacke, argillite and tilloid,

3. Bicholim formations include chloritic amphibole schist, ferruginous pink phyllite and manganese, iron. 4. Vageri formations – include metagrey whacke with minor proportion of metabasalt. The above rock is intruded by granite gneiss, feldspathic gneiss, hornblende granite, and porphyritic granite.

A number of major and small faults and perpendicular weak planes in the west, south-west directions are noticed in the area covered by laterite. The major rivers like Mandovi, Zuari, Chapora, and Terrakhol flow along the weak planes in their last lap.

Over a 3rd part of Goa is covered a mantle of laterite of varying thickness of 10 to 50 mts. It occurs in two levels below 100 mts. MSL and above 30 mts. MSL. The lower level laterite is dated to Pleistocene Period and that which occur in the higher level is dated to the late tertiary age.

Physiographically, Goa can be divided into three zones viz., i) the Ghats on the East forming part of the Sahyadri range covered with thick moist deciduous forest ii) the Coastal plains on the west and iii) the transitional zone in between the ghats and the coast with low dissected hills and table lands (Map 1).

The area along the Western Ghats comprising Sattari, Sanguem and Canacona areas of the state is thickly forested. Patches of forest are also found in Quepem, Pernem and Ponda. Of the total area of the state, nearly 28.41% is under forest cover.

The ghat and the sub ghat region are very rich in forest wealth. The important types of trees grown are *michelia*, *bischofia*, and *rubiacca*, etc. In the high altitude covered with evergreen forest (above 2000mt.MSL), *carrissa*, *vitex*, *grevia*, etc. are grown. The sub ghat region is covered with moist deciduous forest and in the

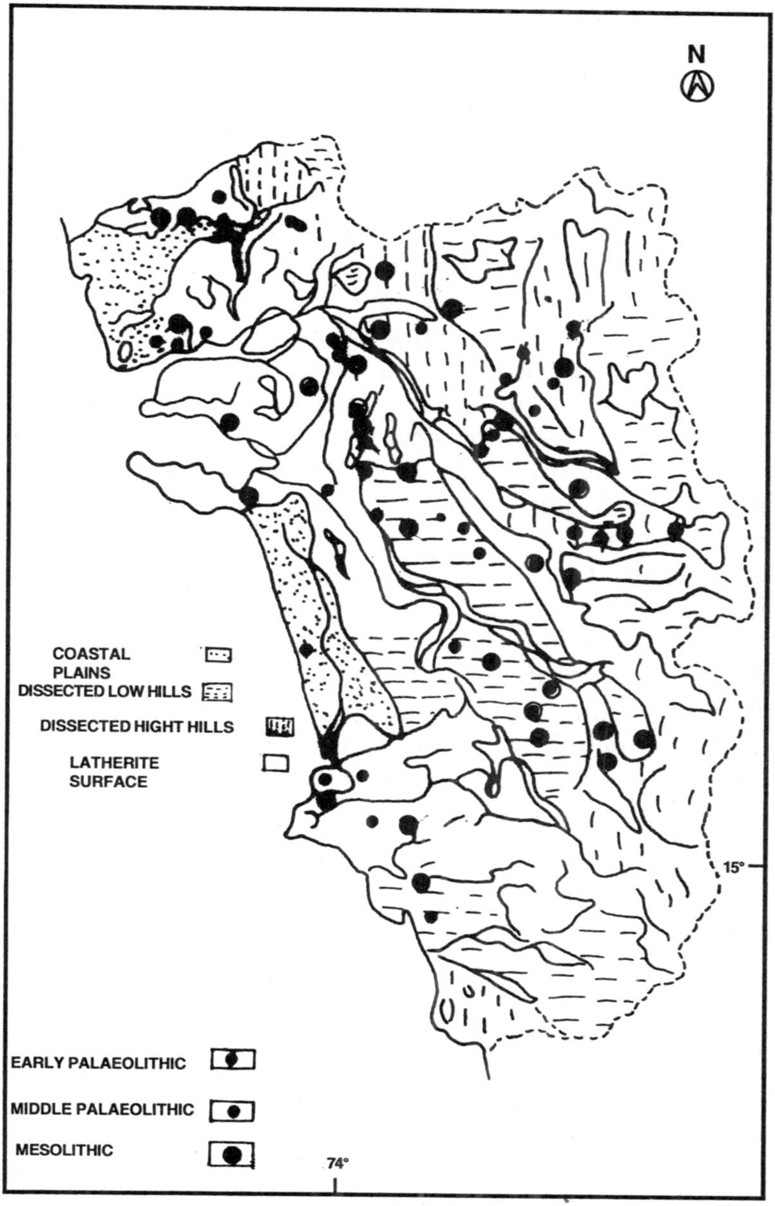

Map 1 : Geomorphological Map of Goa

coastal plains grown are the roots of *rhizophora*, *kadelia*, and trees like *pandanus* etc. The coastal mangroues serve as breeding grounds for marine fish.

The moist deciduous forests of the Sahyadri and the adjoining areas with plenty of rain falls are an ideal habitat for numerous species of animals and birds. The common animals are *Loris tardigradus* (slender Loris), *Panthera pardaus* (leopard), *canis aureus* (jackals), *sus scrofa*, and *Bos gaurus* (Gaur) and various types of deer. Significantly the remains of *rhinoceros decanencis* (gigantic rhinoceros) have been found in the Gokak formation of Belgaum area. Therefore, it was suggested that the gigantic rhinoceros lived in Goa also during the middle Pleistocene (Prasad & Rao 1985). Many types of snakes both poisonous and non-poisonous were found in the area. There are 208 species and sub species of birds noticed in Goa (Saha and Das Gupta: 1992). They belong to 124 genera, 44 families and 15 orders. They include *Ardeolo Striatus* (little green horn), *Cinconoa Episcopus* (white naked stork), *Pernis ptilorhynchus ficollis* (Indian crested honey buzzad), etc. Various types of doves including *Strptopelia Chinesis* (spotted dove) are also noticed in the area.

The denudation of laterite and the parent rocks (crystalline gneiss and metamorphic rocks) have given rise to laterite soil, yellowish brown alluvial soil, red loamy soil and mixed red and black soils in the hilly regions and valleys (Govindarajan: et al; 1974). In the coastal plain sandy soil and dunes are found. Laterite soil, rich in organic content, covers nearly 75% of the region. The soil of the valley is fertile as it is mixed with humus and light sand. The Khazan lands (low-lying land created by erecting embankment to prevent sea water from entering) are covered with silty clayey soil and silty clay loam. They are acidic and fairly organic (Map 2).

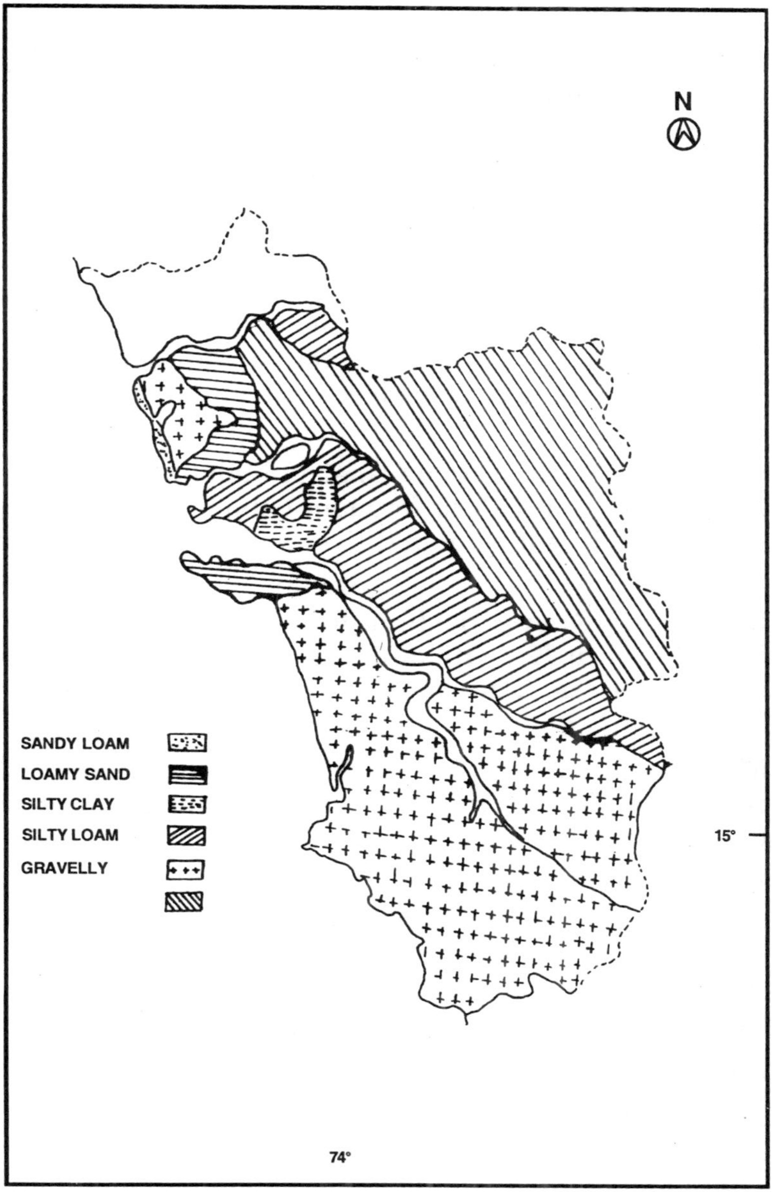

Map 2 : Soil Map of Goa

The region is known for a variety of minerals. Some of the industrial minerals are bauxite, asbestos, feldspar graphite, silica, limestone etc. Iron and manganese are the important ores available.

All the rivers draining the state originate from the Western Ghats either from Karnataka or Maharashtra. The principal rivers and tributaries are described below:

Terrakhol: Rising in the Usappa ghat in Sawantwadi district of Maharashtra, it flows along the boundary between the two states. Its important tributary is Kadashi. It is a perennial river with a tidal length of 26 kms.

Chapora : Rises in Rama Ghat in Maharashtra where it is called river Tillari. Its main tributaries are Kalna and Arabo. It is a perennial river with a tidal length of 32 kms.

Mandovi: Rising in Jambhoti Ghat in the main Sahayadris in Karnataka and it flows 77 kms before meeting the sea. It has two branches, namely, Madai and Khandepar.

Madai: It is a perennial river. It rises in Karnataka and runs about 30 kms in Karnataka and flows 40 kms in Goa. Its tributaries are (1) Surla (2) Veluz and (3) Ragada.

Khandepar: It originates in Karnataka and enters Goa at Dhudsagar waterfalls. Its length is about 65 kms and is also a perennial river. Dabol and Collem are the main tributaries. The minor tributaries are Cunde, Valvat, Bicholim, Assonora and Sinkerim.

Zuari: It is another major river in Goa. The meeting of two rivers, Salauli and Uguem near Sanguem town, forms it. River Salauli runs 34 kms before meeting river Uguem. The length of the river Zuari is 34 kms. Kusavathi is the main tributary of river Zuari. It is a tidal river.

Sal river: Rising in Salcette, it flows to a distance of 40 kms parallel to the coast before meeting the sea at Betul. It is a tidal river.

Saleri river: It rises near Barcem in Quepem and drains taluks of Quepem and Canacona. It runs to a distance of 11 kms.

Talpona river: It rises in the Western Ghat on the Goa side. It has two branches, namely Goundongerim and Cuska.

Galjibag river: Originating from the Western Ghats it flows to a distance of 14 kms in the Canacona talauk.

A notable feature of the drainage system is the Kumbharjua Canal linking the two major rivers, Mandovi and Zuari. Another feature is the occurrence of numerous springs, which are common in a laterite territory. Investigations have shown that the "chemical quality of the ground water is generally good and except where tidal rivers enter into rivulets in the plains" (Desai; 1985; 425 – 30). Some Geologists (Gokul et al. 1985; 2- 21) suggested after considering the number of rivers entering Goa across the Ghat with many waterfalls in their course, the presence of some terraces along the upper reaches of rivers Madei, Sanguem and Zuari rivers and they observed that the western ghat has been subsequently rejuvenated.

Goa receives seasonal rains from June to October from southwest monsoon. The rainfall rapidly increases towards the Western Ghats. The variation in rainfall from year to year is not large and cyclonic disturbances are occasional. The average rainfall is 350 cms. The average minimum temperature is 21°C and the average maximum temperature is 30.9 C. All through the year the climate is pleasant. The relative humidity is about 60%.

Sporadic references to the historical remains in Goa are found in Portuguese documents and journals. Pissurlencar (1938) made a significant contribution by collecting good data on the temples that existed during the Portuguese period. He also referred to a few Kadamba inscriptions that have been transported to Lisbon. He made a passing reference to the Chicalim underground chambers which were later studied in detail by Gritli Mitter Walner. Perhaps Fr. Heras was the first scholar to study the archaeological remains in a planned manner from 1928. His methodical survey and study of ancient remains include sites such as the Arvalem caves, Chandrapura and Gopakapattana, the ancient capitals of Goa, the Buddhist image from Colvale Saptakoteswara temple at Nanora, etc. He collected a large number of sculptures and inscriptions, which are now preserved in the museum at the Historical Research Institute of Bombay. Moraes (1931) made a thorough study of the Kadambas of Goa based on inscriptions and monuments.

No further survey was carried out until 1961, the year of Goa's accession to India. Immediately thereafter the Archaeological Survey of India carried out village-to-village survey as per the policy decision taken by the Government of India under the IInd five-year plan. In 1969, Sundara (personal communication) discovered a site with Neoliths at Tamdi Surla that was perhaps the first pre-historical site noticed in Goa. Sali (IAR 1964-65: 8-10) surveyed and discovered a potential lower Paleolithic site at Shigao besides two middle Palaeolithic sites and 66 Mesolithic sites (referred to as late stone age sites by the explorer). They perhaps include upper Paleolithic sites. The entire collection needs to be reviewed. Almost simultaneously Ramesh carried out Epigraph survey (EI XXXVII; 1966; 282-88) and copied 34 stone inscriptions in Kannada, Sanskrit and Marathi throwing fresh light on the history of Goa. Of this only four are fully published and the rest are listed in ARIE and IAR (1962-63; 49 &1963-64; 68). Gune carried out a preliminary survey of sculptures besides giving an outline of the history and archeology of the region.

Mitterwallner (1971 &1981) carried out a survey of the monuments and sculptures of Goa. She also carried out a careful examination of the underground chambers at Chicalim, the rock-cut caves and temples and tried to trace the development of art and architecture.

Gurav (1969) made an exhaustive study of history of the Goa Kadambas based on inscriptions. He used 135 inscriptions datable from 11th to 13th C. A.D. most of which are from Karnataka and a few from Goa. In 1974, S.R. Rao (personal communication) carried out a trial digging at Chandrapura, which yielded an earlier temple probably of the Satavahana period below the existing one. A large number of pottery and copper coins and ornaments were found in the excavations. Another trial trench was laid at Chicalim near the underground chambers. It yielded pottery (not described), a solitary Neolithic celt and an iron arrow head. (ASI records)

Pereira (1978) did a yeoman service in the field of art and architecture by compiling all the available data on temples, deities, and local beliefs and transfer of deities during the Portuguese period. Rao (1978) found a Mesolithic site at Rivona during the course of his fieldwork. Banerjee (IAR 1979–80) carried out further survey along the coast, with a view to assess the prehistoric environment of the region. His survey yielded 7 sites with neoliths and a few more Mesolithic sites such as Anjuna, Cananguinim, Candolim, Chapora and Nuem. The collection included scrapers, points and borers. A few Neolithic celts, chisels and hammer stones were also collected from Arali. Katti (1980; 2) published a short note on the Arvalem cave inscriptions. Soundararajan (1981; 44-7) studied the Aravalem caves and dated them to 6th century A.D. on stylistic grounds. Explorations in Mandovi and Zuari basins (Marathe; 1983; 87-93) yielded lower and middle Palaeolithic sites at Shigao area and Fatorpa besides a Mesolithic site at Keri.

Kale (1983) made the first attempt to study the Palaeo environment of the region. His investigations have shown that Mandovi and Zuari valleys are carved out after the emergence of the western ghats and coastal strip and are datable to the mid Tertiary. He dated the pre lateritic pebble bouldery gravel to the late Tertiary or early Pleistocene period. Further research in this direction by Dikshit (1983) and Rao et al. (1985) yielded evidence of drowned topography in the lower reaches of Mandovi and Zuari.

The Directorate of Archives, Archaeology and Museum, Government of Goa, reported the discovery of an 'arrow point' from the Kushavati river. But no details as to the place of find, raw material, and tool description are available. The tool is also not available for study.

Dhume refers to one hand axe each from Usgalimol, Anjuna and Thane. These will be discussed in the chapter on Neolithic stage. Dhume incidentally made the earliest reference to the Usgalimol engravings. He mentions "faint line carvings of an elephant and Sun on the rock surface". However, he did not seem to have realized the importance of the discovery.

Shirodkar (1985) reported a large number of Megalithic sites of different types, which include cairn circles, menhirs, cists, dolmens, trilithons, etc. This required further investigations. In 1987 (Shirodkar: 9-15), an important discovery of the image of mother goddess was made at Curdi. He identified it as

Shiroyuktakorravai and dated it to the period prior to the beginning of the Christian era. The sculpture has since been shifted to Verna in view of the threatened submergence of Curdi under the Salauli reservoir Deshpande, (1989).

Kamat (1993) and Shirodkar (1994) carried out a detail study of the rock engravings at Usgalimol and Kazur and dated them to the upper Palaeolithic/ Mesolithic phase i.e. 8,000-6,000 B.C.

The important discoveries of recent times are Acheulian bifaces from Shigao area (Goudellar and Koristtar, 1993: 35-42) and the evidence of Upper Palaeolithic from Molanguinim cave sites (Nambirajan, 1993). Besides these Mahajan (1989) and Mitragotri (1993) also carried out valuable research on sculptures, monuments and inscriptions.

It is obvious, therefore, that the earlier research on the pre Portuguese period has given an outline of the cultural personality of the region. With regard to the Prehistory, ever since the first notice of the under ground chambers in 1938 to 1993 quite a few pre- and proto-historic sites have been reported. But no problem-oriented research has been carried out. A detailed study was required to coordinate all the previous work done in prehistory, to ascertain the problem, to get a working picture of the prehistory of Goa, to identify the promising areas to be explored, to fill up the blanks and to strengthen the less known and to find out its relationship with the environment as also the neighbouring region.

With these problems in view, the entire Goa region was taken up for study with the special concentration on the upper reaches of the major rivers i.e. Mandovi and Zuari. The earlier discoveries have indicated the possible occurrence of primary, lower palaeolithic sites in the subghat region and Mesolithic sites in the central plateau. At the same time efforts were made to locate Megalithic sites and pre-historic natural cave sites in the transitional zone i.e. dissected hills and plateau.

During the course of the fieldwork, a Lower Palaeolithic primary site with Acheulian elements was found at Shigao. Two middle Palaeolithic sites. 14 Mesolithic sites and one megalithic site have been noticed. Of these two are Mesolithic cave sites, three temple ruins, a rock-cut cave of historical period and numerous loose sculptures have also been found during the course of the survey.

2

Early Palaeolithic Sites

Robert Bruce Foote was the first to discover a Palaeolithic tool in India near Pallavaram, Chennai, in 1863. Palaeolithic research in India is, therefore, nearly 140 years old. But it got a real fillip only with the expedition in 1935, of the Yale – Cambridge team, led by H.de Terra and Patterson. They explored the Kashmir Valley, Potwar plateau and Narmada Valley. Burkitt and Camaide worked in Andhra Pradesh. Zeuner carried out an extensive survey in Gujarat. Today the Archaeological Survey of India and a few universities are working on Stone Age archaeology. It is well established now that the Palaeolithic man penetrated into all regions of India including the periglacial sub Himalayas like Kashmir, heavy rainfall areas like Assam and Kerala, semi arid regions like Rajasthan and Kutch.

Generally, the Lower Palaeolithic tools fall into two types: namely, i) pebble tools made by chipping off the upper part of the pebble on one (unifacial) or both the sides (bifacial) and ii) hand axes, which are generally pear or oval shaped and worked on both the faces to give working edges. Though these are the characteristic types, flake tools were also present.

Lower Palaeolithic tools are generally made of quartzite and sand stone. Less favourable material is Dolerite. Rarely, tools made of jasper in Mandasaur, chert in Chikri, phylite and limestone in Andhra Pradesh, granite in Lalitpur area have been found and some metamorphic rocks were also made use of. Considering the fact that the tools are found in different regions of India yet the similar technique and form highlights the fact that the Palaeolithic man handled the varied raw material with equal efficiency.

The important Lower Palaeolithic sites in India are Athirambakkam, Vadamadurai and Gudiam in Tamil Nadu, Nagarjunakonda, Rallavakalan and Yigavari-pallem in Andhra Pradesh, Bagalkot, Tekkalakotta in Karnataka, Nevasa, Mahadev - Piparia in Maharashtra, Lalithpur in Madhya Pradesh, Pahalgam in Kashmir.

The Lower Palaeolithic cultures of India belong to the middle Pleistocene and early part of the upper pleistocene, approximately covering a period of half a million to fifty thousand years B.C.

In the last century, a large number of Palaeolithic sites have been discovered all over India excepting the northern alluvial corridor and Kerala. For the absence of traces of early man in these two regions there could be two reasons. Either, he avoided these areas because of dense forests or lack of raw materials, or the recent alluvial soil has covered the older sites. In other regions Palaeolithic tools have been from plateau, river terraces and hill slopes, therefore, no ecological preferences can be discerned. Kashmir was thought to be devoid of the tools of Palaeolithic man until recently when from there also artifacts have been reported. The picture is obscured by the fact that the known habitation sites are very rare and most of the tools are surface collections from secondary contexts. In fact, they should be termed as occurrences, rather than sites, though following the convention we have also used the word site here.

The Stone Age has been described in various ways, each with its different nomenclatures; series I, II, III; early, middle and upper Palaeolithic; and Early, Middle and Late Stone Age. With the discovery of the Upper Palaeolithic Cultures in India, the term Palaeolithic has been widely accepted and hence used here.

Sali (IAR 1964-65 p.8-10) collected the first early Palaeolithic tool from Goa. He collected a solitary chopper on the pebble from a pebble conglomerate at Shigao. The tool was not readily accessible for study. Later, Marathe (1983) explored the Mandovi-Zuari basins and collected unifacial and bifacial choppers from sites in the downghat region from Collem to Shigao. A descriptive note along with illustrations has been published. Although prehistoric potentiality of the Dudhsagar valley is indicated by the sporadic occurrences of unifacial and bifacial choppers, no detailed study of the region has been carried out.

The area surveyed under the present study is a stretch of 8 km in east – west and 2 km northwest direction along the river Dhudhsagar from Sonavali to Shigao area. Further survey of the region down stream did not appear to be promising. The availability of raw material in the form of pebbles and boulders gradually decreases down stream. Therefore the survey of down stream area was stopped after preliminary explorations.

During the course of the present survey hand- axes, a cleaver, a core scraper, waste flakes and quartzite fragments have been collected from the surface in two sites in Shigao area. Site I yielded numerous split pebbles and worked flakes from the surface. It was noticed that even below surface level split pebbles occur. Therefore, it is suggested that this could be a factory site. As mentioned above Acheulian tools have been collected from the surface at Shigao. Goudellar and Korisetter, (1993 : 35-42) chopper, hand axes, cleavers and flakes from Collem to Sonavali and also at Tambdisurla. (Fig. 1-5)

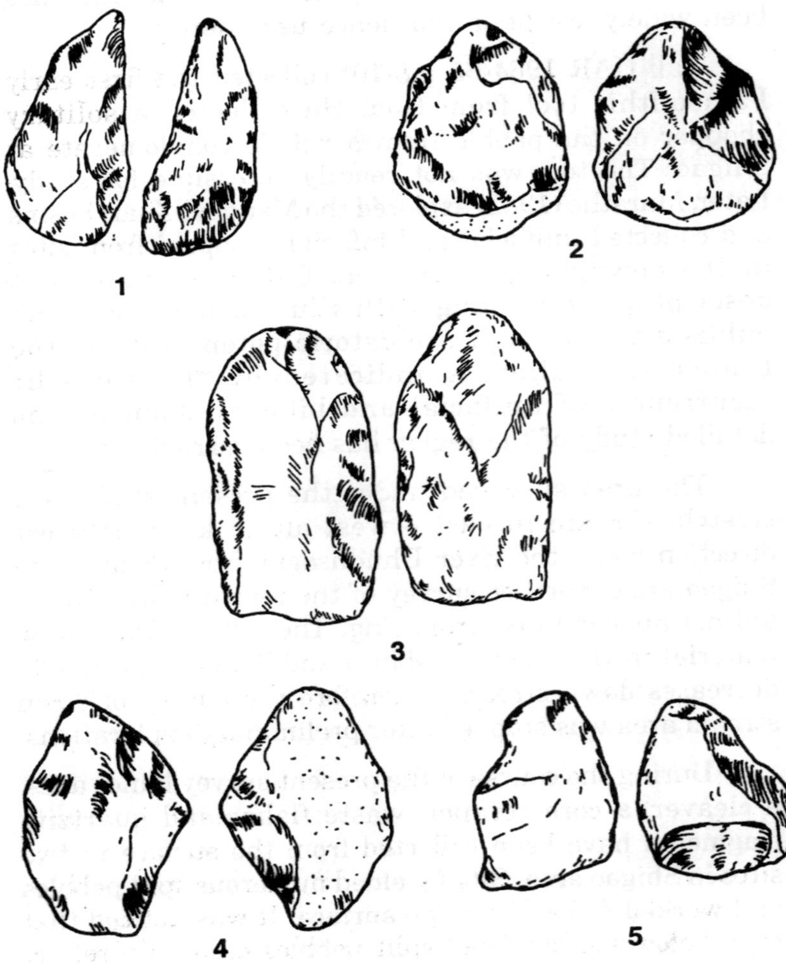

The early Palaeolothic sites so far explored are Shigao, Collem, Bimbal, Sonavali and Tambdisurlla, all located within a radius of approximately 16 sq km. These sites are located on the perennial Dudhsagar River while Tambdisurla is on a rain-fed stream about 8 km north of Collem as the crow flies. It is obvious, therefore, that the concentration of sites is in the Shigao area. It may be owing to three fundamental factors: i) exceedingly favourable perennial water source on considerably large-scale ii) Rich flora and fauna of the region and iii) suitable raw material available in plenty in the form of pebbles of quartzite for prehistoric man to fashion his tools. Thus, Shigao area appears to be the most ideal habitat that attracted prehistoric man.

Exploration was also carried out further north and south of Sanguem in the subghat region, namely, Volpoi and Canacona respectively. In these areas also the environment is more or less similar to that of Shigao area. Tributaries and rain fed-streams, which join Zuari and Mandovi rivers, drain this area. No Palaeolithic tool has been found in this area. It looks as though the big games that could be hunted were more attracted towards Dudhsagar valley and in turn, the prehistoric people were also attracted and this probably explains for provisional non-occurrence of early Palaeolithic sites in the areas adjacent to Sanguem. However, more intensive exploration in future, if carried out, may indicate the truth.

Nearly 56% of the total area of Sanguem taluk is under thick forest cover. The area surveyed is from Sonavali to Shigao along the banks of the river Dudhsagar. The area from Collem to Shigao is located within six kms from the Western Ghats while Sonavali is located amidst dense forest and Tambdisurla is at the foot of the ghats. The moist deciduous forest around

Shigao, Bimbal and Collem has been cleared for cultivation and mining. Small hills are noticed here and there in the vicinity of Shigao area.

The area is very rich in forest wealth. Trees like carissu, vitex, arewis, grow in the area. Plants like cane, bamboo, teak, millets, pulses are cultivated.

The moist deciduous forests of the Shahyadri and adjoining area abound in wild animals. They include slender loris, leopard and various types of deer, jackals and wild boar. Bears are occasionally noticed. The gigantic rhinos (*Rhinoceros decanensis)* found in Gokak and Belgaum, probably lived in Goa during the middle and late Pleistocene (Prasad and Rao; 1985). Various types of poisonous and non-poisonous snakes are also found in the area as also numerous types of birds.

The sites at Shigao, Bimbal, Collem and Sonavali are situated on the banks of river Dudhsagar while Tambdisurla is on a rain-fed stream, a tributary of river Madei. Dudhsagar originates in Karnataka and is a perennial river. (Map 3)

The stratigraphy of Dudhsagar valley, as noticed near the bridge across the river at Shigao, consists of three layers. They are laterite soil at the top (.70 mt); laterite gravel small to medium in size (.80 mt) and at the bottom is the pebble conglomerate (1.8 mt) available in the form of cemented boulders and loose pebbles. They comprise quartzite, flint, dyke, etc.

Kale's (1983) geomorphological analysis has shown that the pebble conglomerate comprises disintegrated materials from meta sediments and metavolcanics. Pebbles are moderately sorted and cemented by ferruginous material on pre Cambrian rocks and are datable to the late Tertiary to the early Pleistocene. Kale felt that the pebble bed probably represents fossil

and secondly the assemblage comprises chiefly of choppers. Although the region between the Malwan and Dudhsagar valley is favourable to the early Palaeolithic people, still no site has so far been noticed in the region. Hence, the possibility of diffusion of Acheulian culture from Malwan region appears to be remote at present.

On the whole, the tool types and technique of tool-making belong to the Peninsular Handaxe / cleaver cultural complex and the Dudhsagar valley seems to represent an outpost in the subghat region of west coast.

Regarding the probable food habits more research work has to be carried out, work of the type done in the Hunsgi Valley of Karnataka (Paddayya; 1980& 1985). The flora and fauna including the big games mentioned above provided food supply to the Early Palaeolithic people. However, direct evidence in the form of fossils is yet to be traced.

APPENDIX - I

IMPORTANT LOWER PALAEOLITHIC SITES

1. SHIGAO I (Sanguem)

- It is about 3 kms west of Collem.
- 15° 20' 02" N; 74° 14' 05" E.
- In the sub ghat region about 5 kms from the foot of the ghats, three layers are noticed near the bridge across the river in the village. They are top: laterite soil 70 cms; middle: laterite gravel small to medium in size 80 cms; bottom pebble conglomerates 1.80 cms.
- Numerous quartzite and flint pebbles and few quartz framents found scattered on surface. No rounded pebbles found in the site. The site yielded no tools. It is a factory site.

- Another site in the same village marked as Shigao-II is about 50 mts west of Sateri temple. The area measures approximately 500 sq mts and is under cultivation.
- Early Palaeolithic tools found on surface. The collection includes 2 hand axes, I cleaver and a few middle Palaeolithic flakes.
- Mesolithic tools on quartz are also collected from the surface.

Other Archaeological Remains

a) In the centre of the site-II, seven monolithic pillars of laterite (dressed) rectangular in section are noticed. They are standing in east west orientation. Locally called Barazan (twelve people).

b) A small rock cut cave with lion sculpture *in situ* was found about 1000 mts north of the site

c) About 50 mts west of the pillars and within the site found is a dilapidated temple of Sateri with a few loose sculptures datable to 16th- 17th century A.D.

2. COLLEM (SANGUEM)

- It lies 3 kms southwest of Mollem on the Vasco da Gama-Londa railway line in the downghat region
- 15 °21' N; 74' 15' 05" E.
- Thick moist deciduous forest in the area.
- Forest cleared for cultivation and mining around the village in recent times. Plain area intercepted by small rocks at a few places. Wild animals like slender loris, Gaur deer, leopard, etc., are found in the area as also numerous types of birds and snakes.
- It is on the banks of river Dudhsagar. Raw materials like quartz, flint, etc., are available abundantly.

- Sali reported Mesolithic tools. Marathe collected unifacial choppers from the area. Luther and Korisetter reported Acheulian bifaces from the area. The present survey yielded no tools from the sites.

3. TAMBDISURLA (SANGUEM)

- It lies 8 kms south of village Surla.
- 15°16' 30" N. 74° 15' 00" E.
- Downghat region.
- The site is at the foot of the Western Ghats. The area is densely forested with moist deciduous forest. The surface soil is laterite. Quartz and quartzite fragments found on surface. The area is under paddy cultivation.
- A small rain-fed stream called *Vazar sakalacho vyal* flows closely.
- Sundara reported a butt end of a Neolithic celt near Tambdisurla. Luther reported Acheulian bifaces. Mahadeva temple of 12th century A.D stands near the site. Shirodkar has identified three vertical slabs standing about 5 mts behind the temple as menhirs. Quartz and quartzite fragments found infrequently on surface. Worked flakes, cores a point, a border, scraper and waste flakes collected from the surface.

TOOL DESCRIPTION

1. Site: Shigao II

   Raw material: Quartzite

   Tool type: Hand axe.

   Description: Pear shaped. Deep flake scars on both sides. Prominent median ridge. Zigzag margins. Patch of cortex retained at the butt. Pointed tip. Fresh. Measurements; 14.0 × 7.2 × 6.0 cm.

2. Site: Shigao II

   Raw material: Quartzite.

   Tool type: Hand axe.

   Description: Triangular shaped. Shallow flake scars on dorsal. Deep and broad flake scars on the ventral. Patch of cortex retained at the butt. Plano convex in section. Zigzag margins. Roundish tip. Fresh. Measurements: 10.8 × 8.0 × 4.4 cm.

3. Site: Shigao II

   Raw material: Quartzite

   Tool type: Cleaver

   Description: U-shaped. Lateral margins almost straight. Thick at the centre. Patch of cortex retained at the butt. A broad flake removed at the ventral to obtain cutting edge. Lenticular in section. Fresh. Measurements: 16.8 × 9.3 × 4.2 cm.

4. Site: Shigao II

   Raw material: Flint

   Tool type: Scraper.

   Description: Made on thick pebble. Broad flakes removed from the dorsal. Ventral unworked. Thick right margin. Convex working edge. Retouched. Measurements 10.7 × 7.4 × 5.6 cm.

5. Site: Shigao II
   Raw material: Flint
   Tool type: Core.

Description: Irregular in shape. Two deep and broad flakes and three narrow blade flakes removed. 60% cortex retained. Measurements 6.8 × 6.7 × 4.6 cm.

3

Middle and Upper Palaeolithic Sites

In the 1930s a distinct flake blade industry based on raw material, typology and stratigraphy was identified in India known as series II or Middle Stone Age and Nevasian. De Terra reported four flake tools from Kandivali and Kurnool regions. Later, similar tools were found in the Godavari valley. Explorations carried out in the last three decades brought to light hundreds of sites in Maharashtra, Karnataka, Andhra Pradesh, Orissa, Madhya Pradesh, Rajasthan, Punjab and Kashmir. A detailed study of the Middle Palaeolithic sites in Maharashtra, Karnataka Andhra Pradesh and Madhya Pradesh, has shown that there are more Middle Palaeolithic sites than Lower Palaeolithic sites. This is probably due to an increase in population.

The major regions where Middle Palaeolithic tools have been found are Belan Valley, Gujarat, Rajasthan, and Singhbhum and Valley in Bihar.

The representative tools are parallel-sided blades, scrapers, points, borers, etc. Burins are rare. There is evidence regarding the origin of this industry, of an evolutionary process stemming from that of the late stage of Lower palaeolithic industries. The materials largely used are cryptocrystalline silica like agate, jasper, chert etc. The tools are generally smaller in size than those of Lower Palaeolithic. In some areas, particularly Madras, Lower Deccan and Kutch the tools of the Middle Palaeolithic age continued to be made of the same material (quartzite) as those of the Lower Palaeolithic but the material for the former seems to have been fine grained and more carefully selected. Thus the collection of the Middle Palaeolithic tools from the different regions does not show uniform pattern of tool-types.

The distinct flake blade industry has been discovered in various parts of the country during the last two decades. The assemblage represents a very defined industry and can be placed between middle Palaeolothic and Mesolithic. The principal tool type are backed blades, lunates, points, awls, etc. The important sites are located in Chittor and Kurnool districts in Andhra Pradesh, Belan valley in Madhya Pradesh, Patne in Maharashtra and Shorapur doab in Karnataka. The excavation at Patne yielded a disc bead made from a fragment of ostrich eggshell. This is the earliest ornamental object from an upper Palaeolithic phase in India. Based on the stratigraphical position of this culture, a date to the end of the Upper Pleistocene and the early part of Holocene has been assigned.

During the course of the intensive survey of Goa region in early 60's Sali (1964-65) discovered two Middle Palaeolithic open-air camp sites at Arali and Fatorpa. The industry included points, scrapers, awls, cores, flakes, and a few blades on short thick flakes. The raw material used was cherty quartz. Later Marathe (1985) also collected Middle Palaeolithic tools from Fatorpa. Thus, the previous work done in the region yielded Middle Palaeolithic sites only and there was no evidence available with regard to the Upper Palaeolithic stage.

During the course of the present study a middle Palaeolithic site was discovered at Anakhane and Pernem besides, Shigao and Molanguinim, which is a cave site. They have provided evidence of respectively a transitional stage of early Palaeolithic to middle Palaeolithic and the emergence of Mesolithic from the upper Palaeolithic. However, no site has yielded evidence clear-cut existence of the Upper Palaeolithic stage in Goa (Figs. 6-15).

6

7

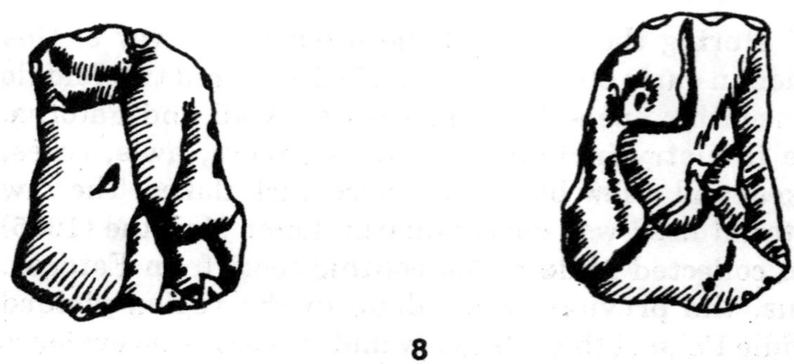

8

9

10

11

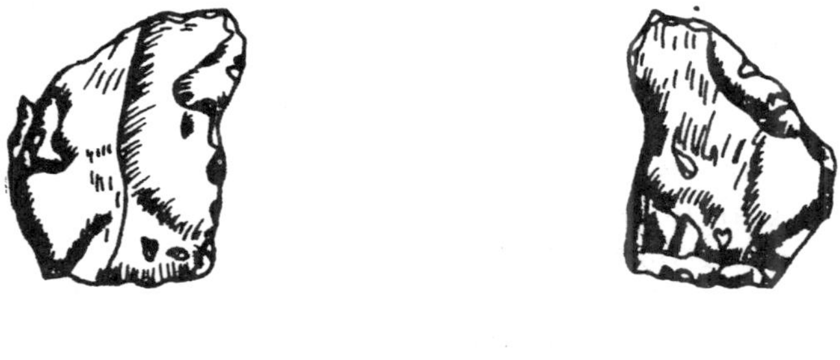

12

13

14

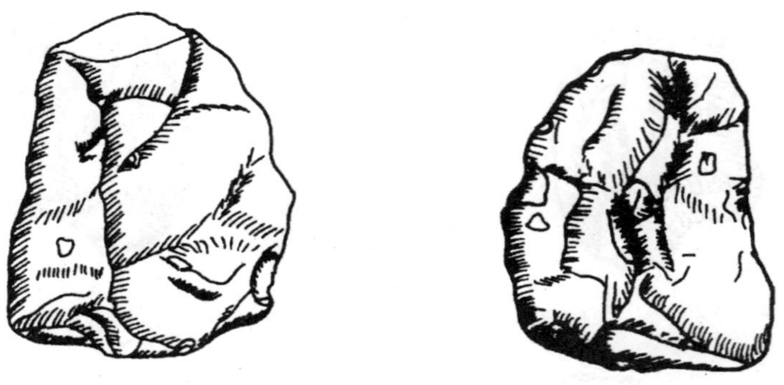

15

Of the two middle Palaeolithic sites reported earlier, Arali is located on a plateau overlooking the sea. On the other hand, Fatorpa is located in an undulated area and is about 5 km from the sea. The newly discovered site of Anakhane is located on a plateau at about 20 kms inland and near the ghats.

Table No. 1

Metrical Analysis of Middle Palaeolithic Tools

Length	No.of Tools	Breadth	No.of Tools	Thickness	No.of Tools
16 – 20	2	16 – 20	4	5 – 9	5
21 - 25	3	21 - 25	5	10 - 20	9
26 - 30	5	26 - 30	3		
31 –35	1	31 - 35	1		
36 - 40	3	36 - 40	1		
Total	14		14		14

Lengthwise 57% of the collection ranges between 21-30 mm. In breadth also 21-30 mm range is dominant. 64% of the specimen has a varying thickness of 20 – 30 cms. (Figs. 16-26)

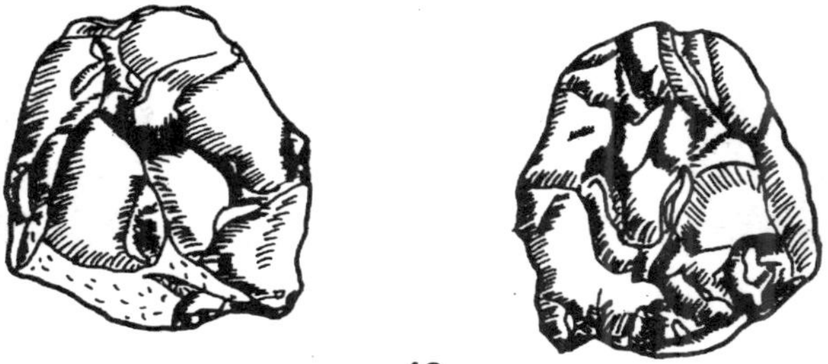

16

17

18

19

20

21

22

23

24

25

26

Shigao, an Early Palaeolithic site discovered above, also yielded evidence of large flakes and cores indicating emergence of the Middle Palaeolithic. It is located about 40 kms inland in the subghat region. The Molanguinim cave site, which yielded evidence of the upper Palaeolithic, is about 8 kms inland.

The rock material used is chiefly vein quartz and occasionally chalcedony and cherty quartz.

The village of Molanguinim (Salcette), located at the foot of a hillock, is about 3 kms south east of Cuncolim. About ½ km towards the north is a small stream called Pairaban. There are many hillocks in the area covered with wild scrubs. The surface soil is laterite resting on laterite rocks, outcrops of which are seen on the surface also. It is on the slope of the hillock at the village that numerous quartz fragments, flakes and cores (both white vein and milky white vein quartz) are found scattered in good number on the surface. No quartz fragments are found at the foot of the hill, but found on the top of the hill and around the cave (approximately 300 × 300 mts.). Most of the material has a laterite soil tinge making them somewhat reddish. In the exposed section of the Pairaban stream near the bridge no quartz material was found. Characteristically, in the rock formations, quartz veins are found all over Goa. Obviously, therefore the Prehistoric man must have spotted out such veins nearby to procure raw materials.

The surface collection from the site is classified into four categories. (i) Waste fragments (2) Irregular cores (3) Irregular fluted cores and (4) Flakes.

Waste fragments are probably the rejects as the raw materials are found to be the most unsuitable and highly brittle. There are almost perceptible fractures, which are a common property of vein quartz that would not allow flaking in the required way. They are found in large quantity on the surface.

Cores of white and milky white vein quartz are found on surface. The material will break with uneven fracture on striking. Consequently, flakes removed are inevitably irregular. Of the many flakes removed probably only a very few could be used. Hence, it is postulated that since the raw material was unsuitable and only one of its kind available, the pre-historic man was struggling to get suitable flakes with laborious efforts.

Fluted cores found are usually in small size. A prepared platform is noticed on a few specimens from which flakes short and not very parallel-sided have been removed serially one behind the other.

Flakes are highly irregular and are of different sizes and thickness with sharp and thick edges. On the ventral side of a few flakes, the bulb of percussion and the ripples are clear. On the dorsal side of primary flaking with negative scar is seen. There are a few thin flakes with the bulb of percussion on the ventral side and a sharp ridge on the dorsal side. Interestingly, one flake is large and almost parallel sided, similar to an Upper Palaeolithic flake.

The above scrutiny of materials indicates that the site probably represents the last phase of the Upper Palaeolithic in Goa or the beginning of the Mesolithic with the survival of the Upper Palaeolithic.

Shirodkar and Mitragotri noticed a natural cave located in the Molanguinim hillock in the year 1989 (personal communication). But the pre-historic potentiality of the cave was first realized only during the course of the present fieldwork in 1993. The cave has two opening facing towards south and southwest. To ascertain whether the pre-historic man used this cave, to know the stratigraphy and to collect only datable material from the section, a small trial pit was carefully dug inside the cave and the removal of the debris was meticulously done. It has cultural debris to a thickness of approximately 60 cm. Laterite gravel, small to medium size as well as fragments of vein quartz with laterite tinge are found from the top to bottom at every level in varying proportion. Interestingly, milky quartz pieces small to medium in size occur more in number especially up to a depth of 20 cm from the top. Also found in this level are six pot sherds of very late period which infact appears to be accidental and not due to any regular occupation of the cave. Therefore, the debris in the cave represents a single culture i.e. an Early Mesolithic period.

During the course of the digging, charcoal was collected in small quantity at a depth of 10cm. Though it appears that the occurrence of the charcoal is not due to regular burning, yet, it is to be ascertained if it is worth further investigations. Along with the fragments of translucent quartz found are flakes, cores and tools of various sizes.

Broadly, the material may be classified into the upper, middle and lower phases. In the upper phase (0-20cm) small to medium sized quartz flakes with medium to big sized pot sherds probably of late medieval period are found.

The flakes small to medium size are more in number not only in this phase (0-20cm) but also in the entire collection. The details of the artifacts are given below.

Upper Phase (0-20 cm)

A careful examination of every flake of small to medium in size reveals that most of them are waste flakes. Infrequently, flake scars on the ventral surface and negative bulb of percussion on the dorsal side are noticed. Of the total collection, only 16 appear to be tools.

They include rectangular scraper (1 no), blade (1 no) burins (2 nos) and point (1 no) with somewhat incipient retouch on one side. A few flakes are very small in size, as if they are forerunners of typical forthcoming Mesolithic stage. Two cores with irregular fluting were collected from this level as also another core with thick flake scar.

Middle Phase (21-40 cm)

In the middle phase, the material found is similar to that of the upper phase. But the quantity is less especially of medium to small flakes. One microlithic blade and four points were collected from this level. One of the points is thick and shows signs of retouching. An elongated flake with a clear scar on the ventral side and fluting on the dorsal side was also found. A flutted core with prepared platform was also met with.

Lowest Phase (41-60 cm)

In the lowest phase, flakes are few in number and contra-distinguishingly they are medium to big in size but comparatively thin, reminiscent of the Upper Palaeolithic blades. There is also a fluted core with prepared platform. The small sized flakes are meagre in number. Two large blades were also found in this level.

Table No. 2 : Depthwise distribution of artifacts
Typological Distribution of tools

Depth	Cores	Flakes	Tools	Total	%
Upper phase 0–20 cm.	11	45	18	74	57%
Middle phase 21-40 cm.	6	27	6	39	30%
Lowest phase 41-60 cm.	4	9	3	16	13%
Total	21	81	27	129	100%

The table-2 shows the gradual increase in the activity culminating in the upper phase. The cave was probably occupied during the late phase of the Upper Palaeolithic and continued to be utilized during the Mesolithic phase. Obviously, the cave site represents the transitional phase between the Upper Palaeolithic and the Mesolithic. A similar feature is noticed at Thakkanahali (Poonacha 1990, 287) in the Malnad region of Karnataka and Patne in Maharashtra (Sali; 1985: 137-45).

Table No. 3
Typological Distribution of Tools

Sl.No.	Types	No.of Tools
1	End Scraper	2
2	Side Scraper	2
3	Scraper cum Borer	3
4	Point	11
5	Point cum Scraper	1
6	Blade	8
Total		27

It is clear from the above table that points and blades dominate the collection. Two burins are also found. Interestingly, scrapers also occur along with points and blades. It may be noted here that in the Upper Palaeolithic phase of Northern Karnataka along with blades and burins, scrapers and points also occur. Probably, the scraper in the collection represents the continuity of the earlier tradition, though smaller in size.

Table No.4

Metrical Analysis of Upper Palaeolithic Tools

Length	No of Tools	Breadth	No of Tools	Thickness	No of Tools
16-20 cm	2	6-10	1	0-4	1
21-25	4	11-15	3	5-9	3
26-30	3	16-20	2	10-20	9
31-35	4	21-25	3	21-25	1
36-40	1	26-30	3	26-30	0
41-50	1	31-45	3	31-35	1
Total	15		15		15

Length range between 21-35 mm is dominant with 73%. Breadthwise there is near equal distribution between 11-30mm. 60% of the specimens vary in thickness between 10-20mm.

Thus, the whole stratigraphy seems to indicate a steady development from the fag end of the Upper Palaeolithic to early the Mesolithic, though not over a long period. (Fig. 27-28)

Therefore, the investigations in the cave and the surface collection indirectly indicate the transition of the Early Mesolithic from the disappearing Upper Palaeolithic. There is no clear stratigraphical evidence and the available tools are meagre to make any definite conclusions. Surprisingly, the finished tools are few and far between suggesting that the cave was a factory site.

27

28

It is also observed that thin flakes and points characterise the Mesolithic phase. The big cores, which are found throughout the deposit, have large flake scars indicating the last phase of the Upper Palaeolithic. A horizontal excavation of the cave is required to throw more light on this important discovery of transitional phase.

Thus, the available evidence shows that the middle and upper Palaeolithic man was able to adapt to varied environment, be it coastal area, or in the subghat region or cave site and also using different types of rock material. Therefore, the site represents two cultural stages.

From the above study certain important points emerge having a bearing on the prehistoric period on the environment. As discussed above, Shigao is an early Palaeolithic site and in the same site are found the Middle Palaeolithic elements. This clearly indicates the use of the site over a long period by the prehistoric people. Such sites may even represent the transitional phase from the Early Palaeolithic to the Middle Palaeolithic stage. A more intensive survey is therefore, necessary keeping this point in view. Another important feature is the adaptation of the coastal environment by the Prehistoric people as evidenced by the occurrence of the sites in the coastal strips. Elsewhere in Mangalore region Early Palaeolithic man settled down in the coastal strips (Rajendran 1987). And near Mangalore, Mesolithic sites are also found. A gap, therefore, existed between the occurrence of the Early Palaeolithic and the Mesolithic stages in the coastal environment. The present work has enabled us to fill in the gap and establish the continuity. In Shigao, the evidence of the Middle Palaeolithic phase has been noticed. The Upper Palaeolithic elements are found in Molanguinim and Anakhane.

Thus, a clear and complete sequence of the cultural stages has been established in the western coast. Another noteworthy point is the adaptation of the coastal strip by the prehistoric people away from the thick ghat region.

APPENDIX -II

IMPORTANT MIDDLE/UPPER PALAEOLITHIC SITES

1. ARALI (Margao)

- It is 8 kms southwest of Margao.
- 15° 08' N; 73° 58" E.
- Coastal Plain
- It is an undulated area and covered with cashew plantations and scrubs vegetation. Laterite gravel mixed with red soil. The area is rich in Manganese ore.

- River Sal flows near the site. Quartz fragments found on the surface.
- Sali found middle Palaeolithic tools. Banerjee collected a few Neolithic celts and hammer stones from the site. During the present study a few middle Palaeolithic cores and flakes collected.

2. ANAKHANE (Pernem)

- It lies 8 kms to the East of Chandel.
- 15° 49' N. 73° 56'E.
- Central plateau.
- The area is undulated. Cashew trees, wild bushes, beedi leaf grow in the area. No regular cultivation is carried out in the area. Brownish clayey soil rests on laterite rock.
- River Tillari flows nearby. Quartz fragments are available in plenty on the surface in large numbers. Large number of quartz lumps and flakes on surface Mesolithic tools infrequent but yielded good collection of Middle Palaeolithic and Mesolithic assemblage.

3. FOTORPA (Salcette)

- It lies 20 kms south of Margao.
- 15 °13' N; 74° 45" E.
- Central plateau.
- It is an undulated area with a few hillocks in the vicinity. Scrub vegetation dominates the landscape. Coconut and paddy were cultivated. Laterite gravel mixed with red soil found on the surface.
- A small stream, a tributary of river Sal, flows nearby. Quartz fragments are found in good number on the surface.
- Sali and Banarjee reported Middle Palaeolithic tools from the site. During the present survey a Megalithic stone circle was discovered.

MIDDLE AND UPPER PALAEOLITHIC TOOL TYPES

6. Site: Anakhane

Raw Material: Milky vein quartz

Tool type: Round scraper

Description: On a flatish flake. Thick at distal end. Deep flake removed at the working end. Flat margins. Measurements 2.6 × 2.2 × 0.9 cm.

7. Site: Anakhane

Raw Material: White vein quartz

Tool type: End scraper

Description: On a flatish flake. Thick at the distal end. A deep flake removed to produce working end. Retouched, flat margins. Flake scars and ripples on both surfaces. Measurement 2.6 × 2.2 × 0.9 cm.

8. Site: Anakhane.

Raw Material: Milky white vein quartz.

Tool type: End scraper.

Description: On a rectangular flake. Thick at the centre and tapering towards the working end. Faintly retouched, two scars on the dorsal. A broad flake detached to make thumb-hold. Measurements 3.6 × 2.5 × 1.5 cm.

9. Site: Anakhane.

Raw Material: White vein quartz.

Tool type: Point.

Description: Roughly rectangular. High mid ridge. Flatish ventral side with platform Measurements 3.6 × 2.4 × 1.4cm.

10. Site: Anakhane.

Raw Material: White vein quartz

Tool type: Core.

Description: Irregular in shape. A few medium sized flakes removed. Measurement; 2.6 × 2.2 × 1.9 cm.

11. Site: Keri
    Raw material: White vein quartz.

    Tool type: Core.

Description: Amorphous in shape. A few irregular shallow flakes removed. Measures 2.7 × 2.4 × 1.6 cm.

12. Site: Anakhane.

    Raw material: White vein quartz.

    Tool type: Notched point.

Description: Made on thick flake. Flatish dorsal side. Deep flake notched on the ventral. Working point. Serrated margins. Measurements 2.8 × 2.0 × 0.6 cm.

13. Site: Anakhane.

    Raw material: White vein quartz.

    Tool type: Borer.

Description: Rectangular flake. A deep flake detached on the right margin to obtain working point. Two notches on the right margin. Left margin and base are flat. Numerous scars all over surface. Measurements 2.1 × 1.6 × 1.1 cm.

14. Site: Anakhane
    Raw material: White vein quartz.

    Tool type: End scraper

Description: Trapezium. A shallow flake detached at the working end to obtain concavity. A deep flak removed to make thumb-hold. Clear bulb of percussion on the dorsal, flat margins. Measurements 2.2 × 2.5 × 0.7 cm

15. Site: Anakhane
    Raw material: Milky white vein quartz.
    Tool type: core.

Description: Roughly triangular in shape. Two broad flakes removed from dorsal. Flatish ventral surface. Straight margin with prepared platform. Measurements 3.9 × 3.0 × 1.4 cm.

16. Site: Anakhane.

Raw material: White vein quartz.

Tool type: core

Description: Amorphous in shape. Broad and bold flakes removed irregularly. Cortex retained at the bottom. Measurements 5.0 × 4.4 × 3.2 cm.

17. Site: Anakhane.

Raw material: White vein quartz.

Tool type: Lunate.

Description: On a small flake. Straight left margin. Curved working end. Shallow flakes, scars on both surfaces. Retouched. Measurements 2.1 × 1.0 × 0.5 cm.

18. Site: Anakhane.

Raw material: White vein quartz.

Tool type: Flake

Description: Roughly triangular. Four medium sized flakes; scars on the dorsal. Flat ventral sides. Measurements 2.1 × 1.2 × 0.5 cm

19. Site: Anakhane.

Raw material: Milky white vein quartz.

Tool type: Point.

Description: On a leaf-shaped thick flake. High mid ridge resulting from removal of two deep flakes from the dorsal. Flat ventral side with bulb of percussion. Broken tip, retouched. Measurements 2.4 × 1.5 × 1.0 cm.

20. Site: Anakhane
Raw material: Milky white vein quartz.

Tool type: End scraper.

Description: U-shaped. A deep flake removed at one end to produce working end. Numerous scars on both sides. Retouched. Measurements 2.7 × 2.0 × 1.0 cm.

21. Site: Anakhane
Raw material: Smoky white vein quartz.

Tool type: core.

Description: U-shaped. Elongated thick core. Three broad and long flakes removed from the dorsal. Medium sized flakes removed from the ventral. Measurements 3.5 × 2.4 × 1.7 cm

22. Site: Anakhane.

Raw material: Milky white vein quartz.

Tool type: core.

Description: Irregular in shape. One broad and a few long and narrow flakes removed. Measurements 3.2 × 2.6 × 1.7 cm.

23. Site: Anakhane.

Raw material: Smoky white vein quartz.

Tool type: Fluted core.

Description: Roughly square. With prepared platform. Long and narrow flakes removed serially. Left margin at base are flat. Measurements 2.6 × 2.5 × 1.9 cm.

24. Site: Anakhane.

Raw material: Milky white vein quartz.

Tool type: core.

Description: Roughly square. Long and narrow flake removed all over with prepared platform. Measurements 2.8 × 2.4 × 1.4 cm.

25. Site: Anakhane
    Raw Material: White vein quartz.
    Tool type: core.

    Description: Roughly triangular. One deep flake and a few shallow flakes removed. High mid ridge. Flat ventral surface. Measurements 3.3 × 2.5 × 2.0 cm.

26. Site: Anakhane.
    Raw Material: White vein quartz.
    Tool type: core

    Description: Amorphous in shape. Flakes removed irregularly. Measurements 3.5 × 2.8 × 2.3 cm.

27. Site: Molanguinim
    Raw material: White vein quartz.
    Tool type: Burin.

    Description: On a short thick flake. A few shallow flakes on the dorsal. Right margin with beak-like edge. Flat ventral surface. Measurements 1.5 × 1.2 × 0.6 cm

28. Site: Molanguinim
    Raw material: White vein quartz.
    Tool type: Burin.

    Description: On a rectangular flake. A few shallow flakes removed at distal end to obtain working edge. Flat ventral surface. Measurements 1.9 × 1.2 × 0.4 cm.

4

MESOLITHIC SITES

The industries of the Mesolithic age suggest a hunting-gathering economy with emphasis on small game and fishing. It generally indicates adaptation to the early postglacial environment. This period variously called as Late Stone Age, Mesolithic or Microlithic Period. Mesolithic assemblages have been found from all over India. Major sites are Langnaj in Gujarat, Bagor in Rajasthan, Adamgar and Bhimbedka rock shelters in Madhya Pradesh, Morhana Pahar, Lekahia, Sarai Nagar Rai, Chopani Mando in U.P., Singhbhum in Bihar; Birbanpur in West Bengal; Kuchai in Orissa; Selbagiri in Meghalaya; Sanganakallu in Karnataka and Teri sites in Tamilnadu.

The year 1964 is important in the history of archaeological investigations in Goa. The A.S.I. took up large-scale conservation work to the Portuguese Churches in Old Goa and other nationally protected monuments in other parts of Goa. An Archaeological Museum was established in Old Goa. It further carried out clearance work around some of the important Churches as St.Augustine, besides, initiating a village-to-village survey of antiquarian remains along with a survey of the inscriptions in the Goa region. It was during the above survey that for the first time pre-historic sites, viz. Early Palaeolithic, Middle Palaeolithic and Mesolithic were found (IAR; 1964-65: 8-10). What is striking is the prolific number of Mesolithic sites i.e. sixty six in contrast to one Early Palaeolithic and two Middle Palaeolithic sites. Fortunately, Sali the explorer has given a good account of his discoveries. Not only this, he analysed the material from the sites and classified them typologically and submitted a detailed report. Unfortunately, his classification is not published. Later, Marathe (1983: 87-93) of Deccan College Post Graduate and Research Institute, Pune, re-examined Sali's sites and also explored the Mandovi-Zuari basins. He collected Early Palaeolithic and Mesolithic tools from a few sites. He also examined the Mesolithic cave site at Keri, Ponda. He felt that there was a possibility of locating more Early Palaeolithic sites in Shigao – Collem area and that the cave site at Keri should be excavated. Incidentally, Rao (1978: 86-90) as the officer of the State Department for Archaeology on deputation from the A.S.I. brought to light one Mesolithic site at Rivona, Quepem.

During the present survey, the Early Palaeolithic site in Shigao area and also the cave site with Upper Palaeolithic and Mesolithic material at Molanguinim, Salcette were investigated. The Mesolithic sites discovered during the present study are listed in table no.5.

Table No. 5

Sites discovered during the present study

Sl.No.	Site	Taluk	Cultural milieu
1	Alorna	Pernem	Mesolithic
2	Bhutkambha	Ponda	Do
3	Farmagudi	Ponda	Do
4	Tambdisurla	Sangueum	Do
5	Quepem	Quepem	Do
6	Shigao	Sangueum	Mesolithic
7	Verna	Salcette	Do
8	Waghli	Ponda	Do
9	Chandel	Pernem	Do
10	Molanguinim	Salcette	Do
11	Rivona	Quepem	Do
12	Bombdimol	Quepem	Do

It is noteworthy that the Mesolithic sites are heavily concentrated in the central part of Goa, especially in the Mandovi and Chapora mriver valleys. And in the southern part, sites are concentrated in the upper reaches of Rachol river and are thinning away towards the lower coarse. In the northern part there are 60 sites adjacent to Karnataka and Maharashtra. The distribution pattern indicates the possible percolation of the Mesolithic culture of western Karnataka and Southern Maharashtra. It indicates the preference of the people for the down ghat area and the middle reaches of the river to the coastal tract. Obviously, this may be owing to the abundance of the animal and plant foods for the farmer as well as availability of suitable rock material for preparing microliths. recent investigation into the Mandovi-Zuari Rivers have indicated that the tidal length of these rivers is up to 20 km from the estruary area (Desai; 1985: 425-29). This may be reason rather more serious around 10,000-5,000 B.C. On the whole, there is a striking burst of population during this period. (Fig. 29-37)

The rock material used for preparing Mesolithic tools in all the three regions, namely, down ghat, middle reaches of rivers and coastal plains, is more or less the same, i.e. coarse vein quartz. Obviously, this is for the simple reason that no other rock material was available for making Mesolithic tools of the required type.

29

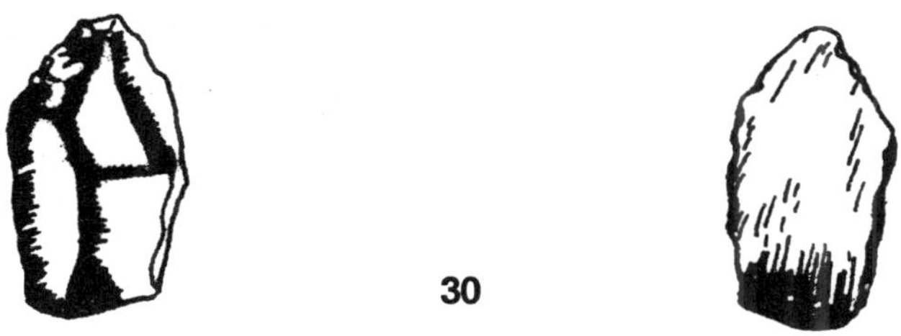

30

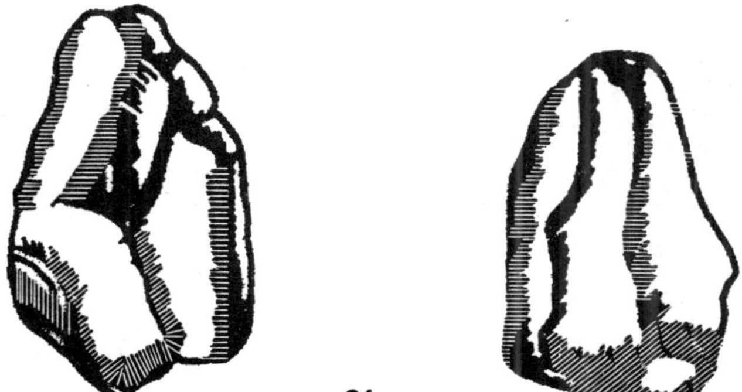

31

32

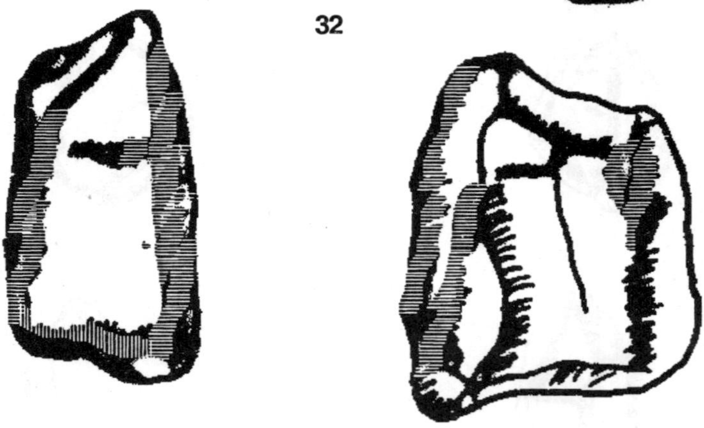

33

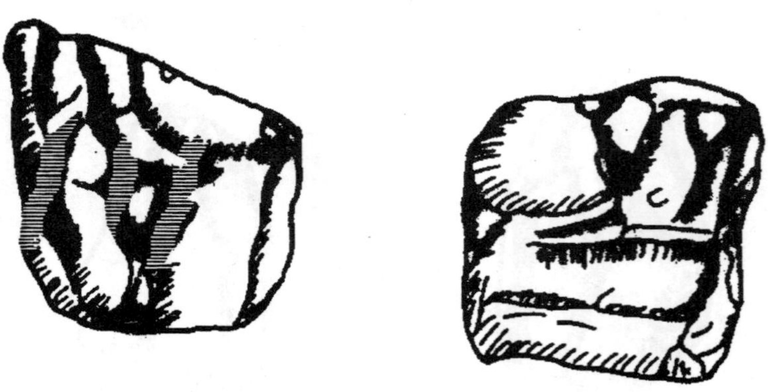

34

35

36

37

Table No. 6

Metrical Analysis

Length	No. of Tools	Breadth	No.of Tools	Thickness	No.of Tools
11-15	8	6-10	7	1-4	6
16-20	21	11-15	24	5-9	42
21-25	28	16-20	37	10-20	38
26-30	24	21-25	15	21-25	2
31-35	9	26-30	6	26-30	2
36-40	5	31-35	7	-	3
41-45	2	36-40	4	-	7
Total	100		100		100

The length range of a specimen varies 11-15mm. Specimens ranging from 16-30 in length dominate the collection with 73%. Breadthwise 61% of the collection is in 11-20 mm. 71% of specimens vary in thickness between 5-20 mm. (Figs. 38-44).

38

39

40

41

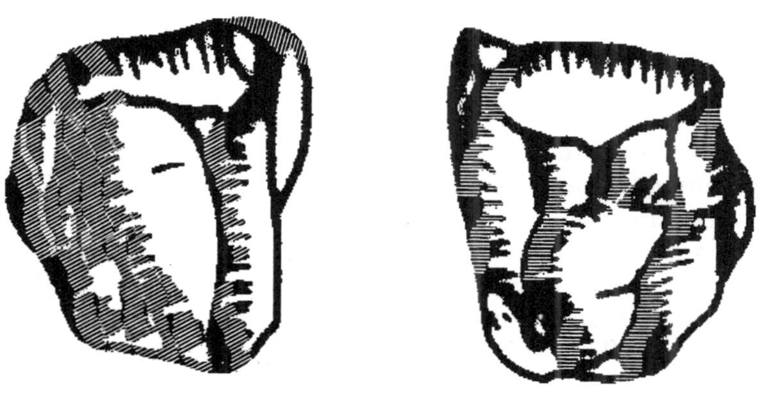

42

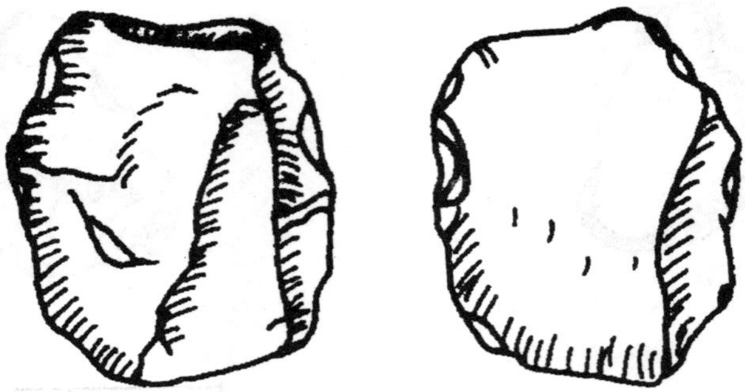

43

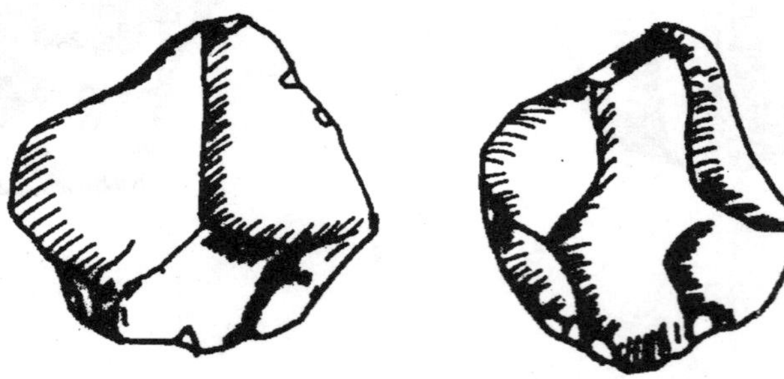

44

It is interesting to note that in the down ghat region usually on the eminence, one may find Mesolithic implements scattered on the surface. It recalls a similar environmental condition of category I sites in the adjacent Malnad region of Karnataka (Poonacha: 1991). In the coastal plains Mesolithic sites occur on the flat laterite surface usually slightly elevated with sparse vegetation. The two different environmental conditions may have their say on the tool types. Future research may throw more light on this aspect.

From the above table certain important points regarding their life style emerge. It illustrates the distribution pattern of the Mesolithic sites in relation to the physiographic divisions. It is evident that the concentration of the sites is more in the centrally dissected plains especially in the major river basins. This concentration can be explained by understanding the environment. The thickly forested down ghat area was probably not favourable for the people with their Mesolithic tool kit. It appears that the less forested central region was more favourable for habitation. Further, the daily tides of the river would bring an enormous number of aquatic creatures, such as crabs, fish, molluses, etc. many of which could be used as food by the Mesolithic people. They could be caught with their Mesolithic tool kit. Besides, fodder grass such as *Isache milliacea*, *Hygroryza artista*, etc., suitable for cattle, grew plentifully in the central region. Therefore, the people could afford to tend cattle (Figs. 45-58).

45

46

47

48

49

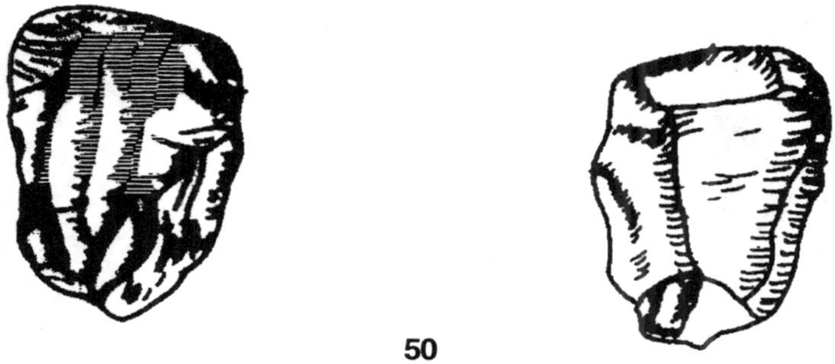

50

51

52

53

54

55

56

57

58

The coastal plains on the other hand, would be extensively inundated during the high tides, and settlement, therefore, in this region was not favourable. There is one more factor to be considered, that is, the sea level fluctuation. Agrawal, Avasia and Guzder (1973,3-7), Agrawal and Kusumgar (1975,146-51), and Guzder (1980), carried out extensive research along the west coast with the help of 'Radiocarbon Age data of Beach rocks'. According to them, the sea level was much lower between 28,000 and 33,000 B.C. Around 28,000 B.C. it rose and receded. It rose again around 13,000 B.C. and attained the maximum level during the mid Holocene. The sea level, they opined, was almost the same as at present in around 4,000 B.C. There was a rise of 1 to 6 m between 4,000 B.C. and the beginning of the Christian era. The work carried out by Kale and Rajaguru (1985,155-68) also broadly tallies with the above findings. Their suggestion of 138 m low of sea level around 10,000 B.C. corroborates with the global sea level curve. They also postulated a steep fall in the sea level from around 10,000 B.C. and reaching almost the present level between 4,000 and 3,000 B.C. Their works showed that the sea level was lower than the present level during most part of the Pleistocene while there was fluctuation above and below the present level during the last 6,000 years. This would imply that between 4,000 B.C. and 500 B.C. the coastal plain was gradually submerging into the sea so much so that it was not possible for settlement. All these factors would account for the heavy concentration of sites in middle reaches of the rivers.

Further, the occurrence of large-sized finished Neolithic celt in Anmod, 10 kms east of Tambdisurla just across the ghat is noteworthy in this context (Bhatsoori, 1990: 81-82). For there appears to be a sort of highway, i.e., a pass from Tambdisurla to Carmali, near Anmod, district Dharwar. The size of this neolithic axe propably suggests an early stage of neolithic phase in the ghat region. (Fig 59-71)

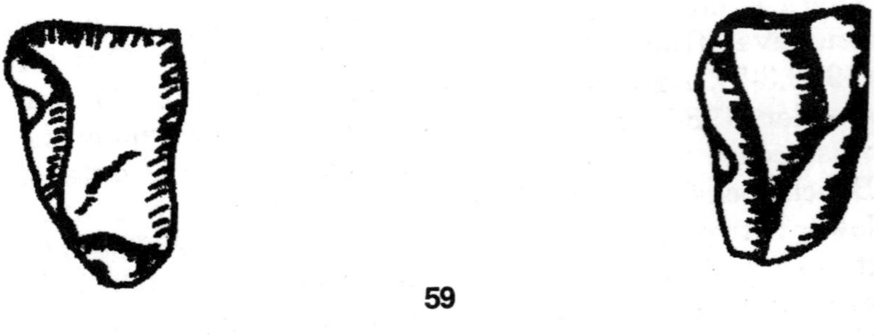

59

60

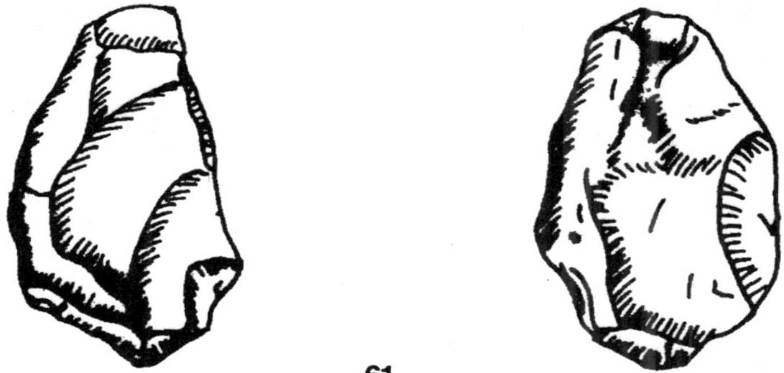

61

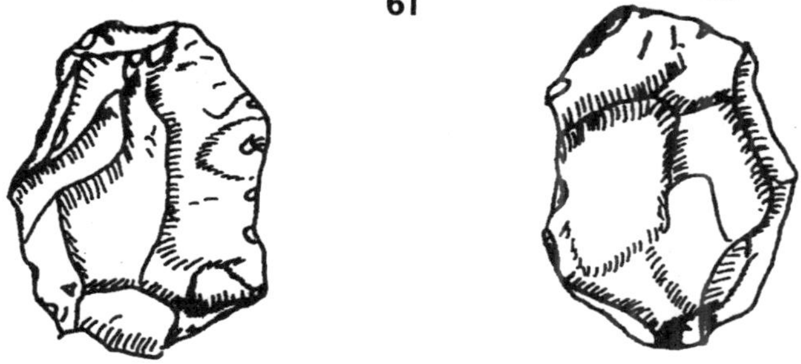

62

63

64

65

66

67

68

69

70

71

APPENDIX - III

MESOLITHIC SITES

CATALOGUE OF SITES

1. PORVORIM (Tiswadi)

- It is located 2 kms north of Panaji.
- 15° 30' N. 73° 49' E.
- Coastal Plain
- It is situated on a plateau. Wild bushes dominate the area. Laterite soil rests on laterite rock.
- No water source is available nearby. River Mandovi flows 3 kms towards south.
- Quartz flakes infrequently found on surface.
- No tools or worked flakes collected from the area. Sali mentioned Mesolithic tools from this village. However exact location is not known.

2. PARCEM (Pernem)

- It is located 9 kms south west of Pernem.
- 15° 40' N. 73° 47' E.
- Central plateau
- The site is on the slope of an elevated land. It is not under regular cultivation. But cashew trees and wild scrubs grow in the undulated area. Quartz flakes and nodules are found moderately on the surface. Rarely agate flakes are found.
- A rain fed stream flows nearby.
- Mesolithic tools made of quartz were collected. Sali reported Mesolithic tools from the village. However, exact location of this site and types are not known. Approximately ½ km to the north east of the village the site is located. The area of the site is approximately ½ × ½ kms. Temples of Brahma,

Mahadeva and other minor deities, sculptures of Brahma, Ravalnath, Ganesa, Gramadevatas are found in the village.

3. VERNA

- It is located 10 kms north of Margao.
- 15° 08' N. 73° 57' E.
- Central plateau
- It is barren land strewn with laterite rocks. Wild bushes and trees grow in the area. Laterite soil mixed with fine gravel rests on laterite rock.
- A rainfed stream flows nearby.
- Shirodkar reports menhirs from the area. Three standing laterite pillars are noticed. The horizontal slab is not there. It is locally called Davornem, meaning load rest. No associated finds are found. It does not appear to be a menhir but may be load rests.

Size	H	B	W
(i)	1.32 ×	0.25 ×	0.41 m
(ii)	1.34 ×	0.21 ×	0.40 m
(iii)	1.34 ×	0.24 ×	0.44 m

- Distance between (i) and (ii) 0.35m and between (ii) and (iii) is 0.40 mts. Alignment is north south. They stand on laterite platform of 2.15 × 0.54 m.

4. QUEPEM

- Quepem lies 48 kms south east of Panaji and 7 kms south west of Sanvordem railway station by road and is used as a Head Quarter.
- 15° 12' N; 74° 04' E.
- Central plateau
- Wild scrubs dominate the area. Paddy is also cultivated. Laterite soil with gravel rests on laterite rock.

- A seasonal stream flows nearby. Nodules of quartz found in considerable number on the surface, which slopes towards the stream. Flakes are also found in considerable number. No quartz material is found in the stream section or the bed, but lumps of quartz material are found scattered in good number on surface.
- Tools are found infrequently on surface. In course of the exploration tools including points, a lunate and a borer, a few flakes and two fluted cores were collected.

5. FARMAGUDI (Ponda)

- It is situated 3 kms north west of Ponda.
- 15° 23' N. 73° 59' E.
- Central Plateau.
- The site is located on a hilltop. Only wild bushes grow on the site and on the slopes of the hill.
- Laterite soil mixed with small gravel on laterite rock. Large quantity of quartz fragments scattered on surface. No water source is available nearby.
- Large number of quartz fragments is found on the plateau and slopes but worked flakes occur sparsely. A few Mesolithic tools were collected.

6. NAGAO (Salcette)

- It lies 10 kms north of Margao on N.H.17.
- 15° 22' N; 73° 55' E.
- Central plateau.
- The site lies on a plateau. It is a barren land with scrub vegetation. Laterite soil and gravel is found scattered on surface.
- There is a natural spring nearby. Quartz fragments found on surface.
- Two standing pillars of laterite were noticed. Shirodkar suggested megalithic affiliation to them.

7. MOLANGUINIM (Salcette)

- It lies 3 kms from Cuncolim towards south and south East.
- 15° 09' N. 74° 15' E.
- Central plateau.
- The scrubs and small trees grow on the hillock. The area near the foot of the hill is under cultivation. Laterite soil rests on laterite rock, which is seen on surface also.
- Quartz flakes are found in good number on the hillock only and not in and around village. The material found at the foot of the hills could be washed-down material. Rivulet Pairaban flows ½ km towards north. A natural spring is also located ½ km south of cave.
- In course of exploration tools were collected from surface. The tools are scattered near the entrance to the natural cave and on the slopes. Natural cave is located ½ km towards west of village. The cave was known earlier. But the archaeological potential was realized only during the present study. Mesolithic and Upper Palaeolithic tools were collected during the present study.

8. DHARGAL (Pernem)

- It lies 8 kms south of Pernem the headquarter.
- 15° 48' N. 73° 51' E.
- Central plateau.
- The area is undulated, rocky area. Wild bushes and cashew trees grow in the area. Laterite soil rests on laterite rock.
- River Chapora approximately 3 kms to the south of the site.
- Quartz material infrequently destroyed found on surface. Sali reported Mesolithic tools from Dhargal village. Exact location is not known.

9. CARAMBOLIM (Tiswadi)

- It is situated 13 kms south east of Panaji.
- 15° 28' N. 73° 56' E.
- Central plateau.
- It is plain area. Paddy is cultivated. Laterite soil rests on laterite rock.
- Rainfed streams flow nearby.
- Sali reported Mesolithic implements from Carambolim. Exact location is not known. No quartz material or tools found during the present study from this locality. A Dravidian Sikara of a medieval temple and a balustrade were found within the village. Small debris noticed in the vicinity indicates the possibility of finding more sculptures.

10. ALORNA (Pernem)

- It lies 26 kms east of Pernem.
- 15° 43' N. 73° 54' E.
- Central plain.
- The site is on the slope of a small hill near the village. Laterite soil mixed with fine gravel rests on laterite rock. Wild scrubs and cashew trees grow in the area.
- River Chapora approximately 1 km away towards south; rain-fed stream nearby. Quartz flakes found on surface in good numbers.
- In course of exploration cores, flakes and tools were collected from the surface.

11. WAGHALI (Ponda)

- The site is situated 2 kms south of Keri towards south west 1 km from Arla crossing on the Priol-Keri road approximately ½ km west of road.
- 15° 30' N. 74° 00' E.
- Central plateau.

- Laterite soil mixed with fine gravel rests on laterite rock. Laterite boulders are visible on surface at a few places. Quartz nodules are found embedded in laterite rock.
- Rainfed stream flows nearby. Quartz nodules are found scattered in good number on surface as also quartz flakes.
- During the course of present survey, cores, flakes and tools were collected from the surface. Plenty of raw material and large number of cores and flakes found. Tools are few and far between. This site is located at about 1 km from Bhutkambh, where raw material is not available.

12. CHANDEL (Pernem)

- It lies 18 kms north east of Pernem.
- 15° 49' N. 73° 54' E.
- Central plateau.
- The area is undulated. Cashew, sugarcane, pepper, arecanut, etc., are cultivated in the vicinity. Laterite soil rests on laterite rocks.
- River Kalna flows ½ km away towards the east. Quartzite, quartz available in the form of river pebbles. Good number of quartz fragments is also found on the surface.
- Mesolithic cores, worked flakes and tools collected infrequently from the surface.

13. BHUTKAMBH (Ponda)

- It lies 3 kms from south east of Keri.
- 15° 28' N. 73° 59'E.
- Central plateau.
- The site measures about ½ × ½ km. It is located on an elevated land. It is a barren land with wild bushes. The area is strewn with laterite boulders

and quartz fragments. Laterite soil mixed with fine gravel on laterite boulders is found on surface.

- A rainfed stream flows nearby. Quartz fragments are found on surface, probably brought from Waghali.
- A natural cave located nearby was reported by the Goa State Archaeology Department. However, no tools are reported from the cave. Marathe collected Mesolithic tools near the Keri cave. Large number of quartz flakes and core found on surface. A few tools and flakes were collected during the present study.

14. COLVA (Salcette)

- It lies 6 kms west of Margao.
- 15° 17 N: 73° 55" E.
- Coastal plain.
- Sandy beaches and headland dominate the area. Laterite gravels and boulders *in situ* are found on the surface. Wild scrub and coconut grooves grown in the area. Quartz fragments found scattered on laterite soil.
- Rainfed stream nearby. Raw material available at the site.
- Mesolithic tools reported by Sali. However, the exact location of the site is not known.

15. PALIEM

- It lies 16 kms west of Pernem, the head quarters.
- 15° 43' N. 73° 45' E.
- Coastal plain.
- Sandy beaches and headlines dominated the area. Laterite gravels mixed with red soil found on surface. Wild scrub growing in the area. The area is rich in iron oar.

- River Terakhol flows half km to the south.
- No quartz fragments were found during the survey. But Sali has reported Mesolithic tool from the area.

16. BAMBOLIM (Tiswadi)

- It is located 6 kms east of Panaji.
- 15° 27' N. 73° 48' E.
- Coastal Plain.
- Plateau and sandy beaches dominate the area. Wild scrubs grow in the area. Laterite gravel mixed with red soil found on surface. Laterite boulders found in large number in the area.
- No water source nearby. Quartz fragments found scattered on surface in considerable number.
- Mesolithic tools collected by Sali. No tool was collected during the present survey. Shirodkar reported one disturbed megalithic stone circle.

17. TUEM (Pernem)

- It lies 7 kms south of Pernem.
- 15° 40' N. 73° 47' E.
- Central plateau.
- It is an undulated rocky area. Wild bushes and cashew trees grow in the area. Laterite soil rests on laterite rock.
- River Chapora flows to the south of the village. Quartz fragments found scattered in the area.
- Sali reported Mesolithic tools. During the present survey no tool was collected.

18. MANDREM (Pernem)

- It lies 13 kms south of Pernem.
- 15° 40' N. 73° 44' E.
- Coastal plain.

- Sandy beaches and headland dominate the area. Laterite gravels and boulders *in situ* are found on the surface. Wild scrub and coconut grooves grown in the area.
- A rainfed stream flows nearby. Quartz fragments are found scattered on laterite soil.
- No tool was found during the course of the present survey, although Sali has reported Mesolithic tools.

19. CUNCHELIM (Bardez)

- It lies 2 kms north of Mapusa.
- 15° 37' N. 73° 50' E.
- Central plateau.
- It is an undulated rocky area. Wild bushes and cashew trees grow in the area. Laterite soil rests on laterite rock.
- Rainfed stream nearby. Quartz fragments are found.
- Sali reported Mesolithic tools. However, no tool was found during the present study.

20. KERI (Ponda)

- It lies 11 kms north of Ponda.
- 15° 28' 30" N. 73° 59' 00"
- Central plateau.
- Area is dominated by hillocks. Wild scrubs and semi-deciduous forest form the geomorphology of the area. Laterite gravel mixed with laterite soil on surface. Quartz fragments found in considerable number on surface.
- River Waghali, the feeder Stream of Mandovi River, flows nearby. Raw material available in the site.
- Sali reported Mesolithic tools; later Marathe also collected tools from the area. During the present survey Mesolithic tools were collected from the site. Tools are collected from the cave also.

21. PILERENE (Bardez)

- It lies 7 kms north west of Panaji.
- 15° 31' N. 73° 47' E
- Coastal plain
- The area is undulated. Coconut and mangroves and wild scrubs dominate the landscape. Laterite gravel mixed with laterite soil found on surface. Quartz fragments are found on surface.
- Rain-fed stream flows nearby. Raw material is available at the site.
- Sali reported Mesolithic tools; however, no tools were collected during the present study.

22. SAVAIVEREM (Ponda)

- It lies 16 kms north of Ponda.
- 15° 26' North 74° 00' E
- Central plateau
- Area is dominated by hillocks. Wild scrubs and semi-deciduous forest from the geomorphology of the area. Laterite gravel mixed with laterite soil on surface. Quartz fragments found in considerable number on surface.
- Rain-fed stream nearby, raw materials available at the site
- No tool was collected during the present survey although Sali has reported Mesolithic tools.

23. NADORA (Bardez)

- It lies 16 kms northeast of Mapusa
- 15° 38' N. 73° 48' E.
- Central plateau.
- It is undulated rocky area. Wild bushes and cashew trees grow in the area. Laterite soil rests on laterite rock.

- River Assnora flows nearby. Raw material is available at the site.
- A few quartz flakes collected from the site.

24. VEREM (Bardez)

- It lies 2 kms north of Panaji.
- 15° 31' N. 73° 47' E.
- Coastal plain.
- The area is undulated. Coconut and mangroves and wild scrubs dominate the landscape. Laterite gravel mixed with laterite soil found on surface. Quartz fragments are found on surface.
- Rainfed stream flows nearby. Quartz fragments were found from surface.
- No tool was collected during the present survey although Sali has reported Mesolithic tools.

25. MACE (Canacona)

- It is located 5 kms south of Canacona.
- 14° 58' N. 74° 02' E.
- Coastal plain.
- The area is undulated. Coconut and mangroves and wild scrubs dominate the landscape. Laterite gravel mixed with laterite soil found on surface.
- A rain-fed-stream flows nearby. Quartz fragments are found on the surface.
- Sali reported Mesolithic tools from the site. No tools found during the present survey.

26. MALCORNEM (Quepem)

- It lies 10 kms east of Quepem.
- 15° 09' N. 74° 02'E.
- Coastal plain.
- The area is undulated. Coconut and mangroves and wild scrubs dominte the landscape. Laterite gravel

mixed with laterite soil found on surface. The area is rich in manganese ore.

- A rain-fed stream flows nearby. Quartz fragments are found on the surface.
- Sali reported Mesolithic tools. But no tools could be collected during present survey.

27. DIVADI (Tiswadi)

- It lies 10 kms west of Panaji.
- 15° 30' 30" N. 73° 54' 30"E.
- Coastal plain
- The area shows signs of drowned topography.
- A rainfed stream flows nearby. Raw material is not available locally.
- Sali reported late Mesolithic tools. However, during the present survey no quartz fragments were found in Divadi area.

28. KURGAON (Pernem)

- It lies 9 kms west of Pernem.
- 15° 40' N 73° 45' E.
- Central plateau.
- It is an undulated rocky area. Wild bushes and cashew trees grow in the area. Laterite soil rests on laterite.
- A rainfed stream flows nearby. Quartz fragments are scattered on the surface.
- Sali reported Mesolithic tools. However, no tools were found during the present study.

29. COLVALE (Bardez)

- It is located 8 kms north of Mapusa.
- 15° 38' N. 73° 50' E.
- Central plateau.

- Undulated area. Cashew trees and wild scrubs grow abundantly. Laterite gravel mixed with red soil found on the surface.
- River Chapora flows one km north of village. Quartz fragments are found in good number on the surface.
- Sali reported Mesolithic tools from the area. Although quartz fragments were found in considerable number, no tools were collected during the present survey.

30. COTOMBI (Quepem)

- It lies 3 kms north of Quepem.
- 15° 25' N. 74° 20'E.
- Central plateau.
- It is an undulated area. There are sugarcane and cashew plantations nearby. Laterite gravel mixed with red soil on surface.
- River Kushavathi flows to the west. Quartz fragments are found on surface.
- Sali reported Mesolithic tools. No tools were found during the present survey.

31. HANATIWADA (Pernem)

- It is located 6 kms south of Pernem.
- 15° 48' N. 73° 49' E.
- Central plateau.
- It is an undulated rocky area. Wild bushes and cashew trees grow in the area. Laterite soil rests on laterite rock.
- A rainfed stream flows nearby. Raw material is available locally.
- Sali has reported Mesolithic tools.

32. TIVIM (Bardez)

- It is located 9 kms northeast of Mapusa.
- 15° 38'N. 73° 50'E.

- Central plateau.
- It is an undulated area. Cashew trees and wild scrubs grow abundantly. Laterite gravel mixed with red soil found on surface.
- Rainfed stream flows nearby. Quartz fragment found in good number on the surface.
- Sali reported Mesolithic tools from the area. Opposite to Tivim Industrial Estate, quartz fragments were met with in good number. A few worked Mesolithic flakes were collected.

33. BONDLA (Sanguem)

- It is located 13 kms north of Sanguem.
- 15° 18' N. 73° 07'E.
- Downghat region.
- It is at the foot of the Western Ghats, which is densely forested.
- River Khandepar flows nearby. Raw material like quartz and quartzite, etc., are available locally.
- Sali reported Mesolithic tools from the site. During the present survey a few worked flakes collected near the village.

34. SARVONA (Bicholim)

- Approximately it lies 2.5 kms east of Bicholim.
- 15° 35'N. 74° 00'E.
- Central plateau.
- It is an undulated area. Cashew trees and wild scrub grow abundantly. Laterite gravel mixed with red soil found on the surface.
- Rainfed stream flows nearby. Quartz fragments found scattered on surface.
- Sali reported Mesolithic tools from the site.

35. CURDI (Sanguem)

- It is located 12 kms south of Sanguem.

- 15° 10'N. 74°14'E.
- Downghat region.
- It is at the foot of the Western Ghats, which is densely forested. The area is rich in iron ore.
- River Salauli flows at the site. Quartz fragments found scattered on surface.
- Mesolithic tools reported by Sali. During the present survey worked flakes and cores of Mesolithic phase were collected. Megalithic stone circles were also found in the vicinity.
- The sculpture of mother goddess was found near the stone circles. Mahadeva temple of 10th-11th century A.D. was located near the village.

36. MOLLEM (Sanguem)

- It is located 39 kms northeast of Sanguem.
- 15°18' N. 74° 14'E.
- Downghat region.
- It is at the foot of the Western Ghats, which is densely forested. Iron ore deposits are found nearby.
- Rain-fed stream flows nearby. Quartz is found abundantly.
- Sali reported Mesolithic tools from the region. During present survey a few worked flakes noticed.

37. MARCEL (Ponda)

- It lies 16 kms east of Ponda.
- 15° 31'N. 73°57' E.
- Central plateau.
- Many hillocks are noticed in the area. The hills are covered with scrub vegetation. Coconut groves and rice are cultivated in the area.
- Many streams bisect the whole area. Quartz materials were found on flat hilltops and slopes.

- Mesolithic tools were reported by Sali; however no tools were found during the present survey.

38. CANDOLA (Ponda)

- It lies 8 kms north of Ponda.
- 15°31' N. 73°58' E.
- Central plateau.
- Many hillocks are noticed in the area. The hills are covered with scrub vegetation. Coconut groves and rice are cultivated in the area.
- Many streams bisect the whole area. Quartz materials were found on flat hilltops and slopes.
- Mesolithic tools were reported by Sali; however no tools were found during the present survey.

39. AMONA (Ponda)

- It lies 20 kms north of Ponda.
- 15° 30'N. 74° 00'E.
- Central plateau.
- Many hillocks are noticed in the area. The hills are covered with scrub vegetation. Coconut groves and rice are cultivated in the area.
- Many streams bisect the whole area. Quartz materials were found on flat hilltops and slopes.
- Mesolithic tools were reported by Sali; however no tools were found during the present survey.

40. VOLVOI (Ponda)

- It is situated 19 kms north of Ponda.
- 15° 31'N. 74° 01'E.
- Central plateau.
- Many hillocks are noticed in the area. The hills are covered with scrub vegetation. Coconut groves and rice are cultivated in the area. Many streams bisect the whole area. Quartz materials were found on flat

hilltops and slopes.

- Mesolithic tools were reported by Sali; however no tools were found during the present survey.

41. PRIOL (Ponda)

- It lies 15 kms north of Ponda.
- 15° 26'N. 73° 59'E.
- Central plateau.
- The village is surrounded by hills. The valley is fertile and arecanut, banana, cashew, paddy, jackfruits are cultivated in the area. Laterite gravel mixed with red soil found on surface.
- Rainfed stream flows nearby. Fragments of quartzite found scattered on surface in good number.
- Although Sali reported Mesolithic tools from the area, no implements were found during the present survey.

42. BANDORA (Ponda)

- It is located 3 kms west of Ponda.
- 15°24' N. 73°58' E.
- Central plateau.
- The village is surrounded by hills. The valley is fertile and arecanut, banana, cashew, paddy, jackfruit trees are cultivated in the area. Laterite gravel mixed with red soil found on surface.
- A rainfed stream flows nearby. Fragments of quartzite found scattered on surface in good number.
- Although Sali reported Mesolithic tools from the area, no implements were found during the present survey.

43. KHANDEPAR (Ponda)

- It lies 5 kms of Ponda.
- 15° 25' N. 73° 03" E.
- Central plateau.
- The village is surrounded by hills. The valley is fertile and arecanut, banana, cashew, paddy, jackfruits are cultivated in the area. Laterite gravel mixed with red soil found on surface.
- A rainfed stream flows nearby. Fragments of quartzite found scattered on surface in good number.
- Although Sali reported Mesolithic tools from the area, no implements were found during the present survey.

44. DABOLIM (Marmugao)

- It lies 6 kms east of Marmugao.
- 15° 23'N. 73° 51'E.
- Coastal plain.
- It is on the slopes of a tableland covered with scrub vegetation. Laterite gravel mixed with red soil found on surface. Laterite boulders are seen in the locality.
- Rainfed stream flows nearby, quartz fragments found on the surface.
- Sali reported Mesolithic tools from the site. No tool was found during the present survey.

45. NAKERI (Quepem)

- It lies 4 kms southeast of Betul.
- 15°09'N. 74° 00'E.
- Coastal plain.
- It is an undulated area, covered with cashew plantations and scrubs vegetation. Laterite gravel mixed with red soil.

- River Sal flows closeby. There is also a spring nearby. Quartz fragments found on the surface.
- Sali found Mesolithic tools.

46. CUNCOLIM (Salcette)

- It is located 13 kms south of Margao.
- 15°09' N. 74° 01'E.
- Central plateau.
- Plain area, devoid of hillocks, characterized by scrub jungles. Paddy, casuarinas, etc., are cultivated in the area. Laterite gravel mixed with red soil found on the surface.
- A stream called Pairaban flows nearby. Quartz fragments found on the surface.
- Sali found Mesolithic tools. During the present survey no tools encountered.

47. XELDEM (Quepem).

- It lies 3 kms south of Quepem.
- 15° 12' N. 74° 04' E.
- Central plateau.
- Laterite soil with gravel on laterite rock. Nodules of quartz found in considerable number on the surface, which slopes towards the seasonal stream. Flakes are also found in considerable number Quartz material is found in the stream section or the bed, but lumps of quartz material are found scattered in good number on surface.
- Rainfed stream flows nearby. Quartz fragments found on the surface.
- Sali collected Mesolithic tools from the site. During the present study a few worked flakes and fragments collected.

48. BETORA (Ponda)

- It lies 4 kms south of Ponda.

- 15° 23'N. 74° 01'E.
- Central plateau.
- Located on a hilltop. Only wild bushes grow on the site and on the slopes of the hill.
- Laterite soil mixed with small gravel on laterite rock. Large quantity of quartz fragments scattered on surface.
- Sali found Mesolithic tools from the site.

49. NAGAVE (Quepem)

- It lies 8 kms southeast of Quepem.
- 15° 20'N. 74° 50'E.
- Central plateau.
- Nodules of quartz found in considerable number on the surface, which slopes towards the seasonal stream. Flakes are also found in considerable number. No quartz material is found in the stream section or the bed, but lumps of quartz material are found scattered in good number on surface.
- Rainfed stream flows nearby. Quartz fragments are found on surface.
- Sali found Mesolithic tools from the site.

50. CONCEM (Ponda)

- It lies 12 kms southeast of Ponda.
- 15° 21' N. 74° 02' E.
- Central plateau.
- Located on a hilltop. Only wild bushes grow on the site and on the slopes of the hill.
- Laterite soil mixed with small gravel found on surface. A large quantity of quartz fragments scattered in the site.
- Sali found Mesolithic tools from the site.

51. MORPIRLA (Quepem)

- It is located 18 kms south of Quepem.
- 15° 08' 15" N. 74° 00'E.
- Central plateau.
- It is an undulated area with a few hillocks in the vicinity. Scrub vegetation dominates the landscape. Coconut groves and paddy were cultivated. Laterite gravel mixed with red soil found on the surface.
- A rainfed stream flows nearby and quartz fragments found in the site.
- Sali found Mesolithic tools from the site.

52. GAUNDONGREM (Canacona)

- It lies 14 kms to the southeast of Canacona.
- 15° 40' N. 74° 39'E.
- Downghat region.
- It is located near the Western Ghats, which is densely forested.
- A rainfed stream flows nearby. Quartz and quartzite fragments found on surface. Found Mesolithic tools from the site.

53. TORXEM (Pernem)

- It lies 14 kms to the north Pernem.
- 15° 46' N. 73° 48'E.
- Central plateau.
- It is an undulated rocky area. Wild bushes and cashew trees grow in the area. Laterite soil rests on laterite rock.
- River Terakhol flows approximately 1 km to the north of the site. Quartz material infrequently found on surface tools nil.
- Sali reported Mesolithic tools from this village. Exact location is not known. North of the Mauli

temple quartz fragments are also found on the surface. However, no tool was found during the present study.

54. HONDA (Volpoi)

- It lies 12 kms west of Volpoi.
- 15°32' N. 74° 02'E.
- Downghat region.
- Thickly forested and rich in iron ore. Semi-evergreen forest dominates the area.
- River Madeil flows closeby. Quartz fragments found on surface.
- Sali found Mesolithic tools from the site. However, exact location is not known. Opposite the Goa Automobile Corporation, quartz fragments are found scattered on the surface. Typical Mesolithic specimens were collected.

55. NANUZ (Volpoi)

- It lies 3 kms south of Volpoi.
- 15°30' N. 74° 04' E.
- Subghat region.
- Thickly forested and rich in iron ore. Semi-evergreen forest dominates the area.
- River Madeil flows closeby. Quartz fragments found on surface.
- Sali found Mesolithic tools from the site.

56. ADVAI (Volpoi)

- It lies 7 kms south of Volpoi.
- 15° 06' N. 74° 00'E.
- Subghat region.
- Thickly forested and rich in iron ore. Semi evergreen forest dominates the area. River Madel flows closeby. Quartz fragments found on surface.
- Sali found Mesolithic tools from the site.

57. VELAGE (Volpoi)

- The village is located 16 kms east of Volpoi.
- 15° 00' N. 74° 08'E.
- Downghat region.
- Thickly forested and rich in iron ore. Semi-evergreen forest dominates the area.
- River Madeil flows closeby. Quartz fragments found on surface.
- Sali found Mesolithic tools from the site.

58. KHADKI (Volpoi)

- It lies 3 kms south of Volpoi.
- 15° 31' N. 74° 04'E.
- Downghat region.
- Thickly forested and rich in iron ore. Semi-evergreen forest dominates the area.
- River Madeil flows closeby. Quartz fragments found on surface.
- Sali found Mesolithic tools from the site.

59. DHANSE (Volpoi)

- It lies 7 kms south of Volpoi.
- 15°28 'N. 74°00' E.
- Subghat region.
- Thickly forested and rich in iron ore. Semi-evergreen forest dominates the area.
- A rainfed stream flows closeby. Quartz fragments are found on surface.
- Sali found Mesolithic tools from the site.

60. CONQUERIM (Volpoi)

- It lies 10 kms south of Volpoi.
- 15°27' N. 74° 05'E.
- Subghar region
- Thickly forested and rich in iron ore. Semi-evergreen forest dominates the area.

- Rainfed stream flows closeby. Quartz fragments found on surface.
- Sali found Mesolithic tools from the site

61. AGLOT (Sanguem)

- It lies 31 kms north of Sanguem.
- 15° 18'N. 74° 03'E.
- Subghat region.
- Thickly forested and rich in iron ore. Semi-evergreen forest dominates the area.
- Rainfed stream flows closeby. Pebble bed found on the river.
- Quartz fragments found on surface.
- Sali found Mesolithic tools from the site.

62. SANCORDEM (Sanguem)

- It lies 33 kms north of Sanguem.
- 15°00' N. 74° 08'E.
- Downghat region.
- The area is thickly forested with a few hills in the vicinity. Iron ore is available in the area. Laterite soil mixed with gravel on surface.
- River Madel flows through the village. Pebble bed of the river provides raw material.
- Sali reported Mesolithic tools from the area. During the present study a few typical Mesolithic specimens and a solitary worked flake, which may represent the beginning of the Neolithic phase, were collected.

63. SANGOD (Sanguem)

- It lies 5 kms west of Shigao.
- 15° 21' N. 74° 10' E.
- Downghat region.
- Thickly forested and close to western ghat.

- River Khandepar flows closeby. River pebbles and quartz fragments found abundantly.
- Sali found Mesolithic tools from the site.

64. CODLI (Sanguem)

- It lies 5 kms west of Shigao.
- 15°21'N. 74° 20'E.
- Downghat region.
- Thickly forested and close to western ghat.
- River Khandepar flows closeby. River pebbles and quartz fragments found abundantly.
- Sali found Mesolithic tools from the site.

65. CORMONEM (Sanguem)

- It lies 8 kms south west of Shigao.
- 15° 12' N. 73° 57' E.
- Downghat region.
- Thickly forested and close to western ghat.
- River Khandepar flows closeby. River pebbles and quartz fragments are found abundantly.
- Sali found Mesolithic tools from the site.

66. VILIENA (Sanguem)

- It is located 18 kms southeast of Sanguem
- 15°09'N. 74° 00' E.
- Downghat region.
- It is at the foot of the Western Ghats, which is densely forested. The area is rich in iron ore.
- River Salauli flows nearby. Quartz fragments are found scattered on surface.
- Mesolithic tools reported by Sali.

67. GANJE (Ponda)

- It is located 20 kms northeast of Ponda.
- 15° 28' N. 74° 05'E.

- Downghat region.
- It is at the foot of the Western Ghats, which is densely forested.
- River Khandepar flows nearby. Raw material like quartz and quartzite, etc., are available locally.
- Sali reported Mesolithic tools from the site.

MESOLITHIC TOOL TYPES

29. Site: Molanguinim (SUR)

Raw material: White vein quartz

Tool type: Flake

Description: Roughly oval-shaped. Three medium sized flutings on the dorsal side. Bulb of percussion on ventral side. Measurements 2.4 × 1.2 × 1.

30. Site: Molanguinim (T)

Raw material: White vein quartz

Tool type: Flake.

Description: Elongated. Two long and two medium sized flakes removed on dorsal. Serrated margins. Flat ventral sides. Measurements 3.1 × 1.8 × 0.5 cm

31. Site: Molanguinim (T)

Raw material: White vein quartz

Tool type: Fluted core.

Description: Roughly triangular. Typical blade core. At least six blades removed. Measurements 2.9 × 1.8 × 1.2 cm.

32. Site: Molanguinim (T)

Raw material: White vein quartz.

Tool type: Flake.

Description: Roughly triangular. Four flakes scars on the dorsal. Flatish ventral and base. Pointed tip. Measurements 2.5 × 1.3 × 0.9 cm.

33. Site: Molanguinim (T)

Raw material: White vein quartz

Tool type: core

Description: Roughly square. One broad and a few narrow flakes removed with platform. Measurements 2.0 × 1.8 × 1.6 cm

34. Site: Molanguinim (T)

Raw material: White vein quartz.

Tool type: Fluted core

Square in shape. A deep and a few small flakes removed. Top and base are flat. Measurements 2.3 × 2.0 × 1.4 cm.

35. Site Molanguinim (SUR)

Raw material: White vein quartz.

Tool type: Flake.

Description: Roughly rectangular. Low medium ridge. Diffused bulb on the ventral. Measurements 2.4 × 1.5× 0.6 cm.

36. Site: Molanguinim (T)

Raw material: White vein quartz.

Tool type: Fluted core.

Description: Roughly triangular. With platform. Two broad and a few narrow flakes removed. Measurements 2.8 × 1.8 × 1.2 cm.

37. Site: Molanguinim (T)

Raw material: White vein quartz.

Tool type: Fluted core.

Description: Roughly triangular. Two broad and a few narrow flakes removed. With platform. Measurements 1.8 × 1.5 × 0.9 cm.

38. Site: Molanguinim (T)

Raw material: White vein quartz.

Tool type: Point.

Description: Roughly rectangular. oblique flake removed at the shorter axis to obtain the point. Retouched. Measurements 2.6 × 1.4 × 0.6 cm.

39. Site: Molanguinim (T)

Raw material: White vein quartz.

Tool type: Point

Description. Roughly triangular. Numerous scars on the dorsal. Clear bulb on the ventral. Pointed tip. Measurements 2.3 × 1.6 × 0.4 cm.

40. Site: Molanguinim (T)

Raw material: White vein quartz.

Tool type: Point.

Description: Roughly triangular. One deep flake each removed from either side towards working edge. Cortex retained at the edge. Measurements 2.4 × 2.1 × 0.6 cm

41. Site: Shigao-I

Raw material: Cherty quartz.

Tool type: Flake.

Description: Roughly square. Shallow flutings on both sides, with platform. Measurements 1.8 × 1.8 × 1.0 cm.

42. Site: Shigao-I

Raw material: White vein quartz.

Tool type: Fluted core

Description: Roughly square. Shallow flakes removed all around. With faceted platform. Measurements 1.8 × 1.7× 1.2 cm.

43. Site: Shigao-I

Raw material: Cherty quartz

Tool type: Flake

Description: Roughly triangular thick end flake. Fluting on the dorsal. Two large flakes scars on the ventral. Measurements 4.2 × 3.8 × 2.1 cm.

44. Site: Anakhane

Raw material: White vein quartz.

Tool type: Backed blade.

Description: On a small rectangular flake. Working end obtained by detached. A steep flake on the right margin. Blunt left margin. Diffused median ridge. Flat ventral side.

45. Site: Anakhane

Raw material: White vein quartz

Tool type: Borer-cum-scraper.

Description: On a thin rectangular flake. Two removed at one end of the longer axis to produce borer. The other longer axis is retouched to produce scraper. Measurements 1.4 × 1.6 × 0.6 cm.

46. Site: Anakhane

Raw material: Milky white vein quartz.

Tool type: Blade.

Description: Parallel, sided diffused median ridge. Flatish ventral side. Wavy Margin. Measurements 1.6 × 1.5 × 0.5.

47. Site: Anakhane.

Raw material: White vein quartz.

Tool type: Bladish flake.

Description: Rectangular flake. Two narrow scars on the dorsal. Depressed ventral sided. Measurements 2.1 × 1.6 × 0.7 cm.

48. Site: Anakhane

Raw material: White vein quartz.

Tool type: Blade.

Description: One elongated flake. Prominent median ridge. Serrated working edge. Retouched. Measurements 2.4 × 1.8 × 0.3 cm.

49. Site: Arali

Raw material: White vein quartz.

Tool type: Flake.

Description: Roughly rectangular. Low median ridge. Diffused bulb on the ventral. Measurements 2.7 × 2.0 × 1.0 cm.

50. Site: Arali

Raw material: White vein quartz.

Tool type: Flake.

Description: Roughly square. Four blade flakes removed serially on the dorsal. Few shallow flakes removed on the ventral. Measurements 1.7 × 1.4 × 0.7 cm.

51. Site: Arali

Raw material: White vein quartz

Tool type: Flake.

Description: Roughly square. Slopy and high ridge on the dorsal. Flat ventral side. Measurements 2.0 × 1.4 × 0.4 cm.

52. Site: Arali.

Raw material: White vein quartz.

Tool type: Flake.

Description: Roughly rectangular. Two broad and a few flake scars on the dorsal. Diffused bulb on the ventral. Measurements 2.6 × 2.0 × 1.0 cm.

53. Site: Anakhane

Raw material: White vein quartz.

Tool type: Blade.

Description: On a small thin flake. Parallel-sided. Low median ridge. Retouched along the margin. Flat ventral side. Measurements 1.2 × 0.6 × 0.3 cm.

54. Site: Anakhane

Raw material: White vein quartz.

Tool type: Blade.

Description: On a short thin flake. Parallel-sided.

Prominent median ridge. Depressed ventral side. Measurements 1.8 × 0.6 × 0.4 cm.

55. Site: Anakhane

Raw material: Milky white vein quartz.

Tool type: Blade.

Description: Roughly square. Parallel-sided. Low median ridge. Uneven ventral-sided. Faintly retouched. Broken specimen. Measurements 1.4 × 1.3 × 0.4cm.

56. Site: Anakhane

Raw material: Smoky white vein quartz.

Tool type: Blade

Description: On a short thin flake. Parallel-sided. Two shallow flake scars on the dorsal. Low but prominent median ridge. Straight left margin and serrated right margin. Flat ventral side. Measurements 1.2 × 0.8 × 0.3 cm.

57. Site: Anakhane

Raw material: Milky white vein quartz.

Tool type: Blade.

Description: On squarish flake. Parallel-sided. Diffused mid ridge. Bulb of percussion on the ventral side. Retouched along the margins. Measurements 2.1 × 1.7 × 0.6 cm.

58. Site: Anakhane.

Raw material: White vein quartz.

Tool type: Bladish flake

Description: Small thin flake. Fluting on dorsal side. Flat ventral surface. Wavy margins. Measurements 1.5 × 0.8 × 0.5 cm

59. Site: Anakhane

Raw material: White vein quartz.

Tool type: Bladish flake.

Description: Small thin flake. Fluting on dorsal side.

Diffused bulb on the ventral surface. Measurements 1.7 × 1.4 × 0.4 cm.

60. Site: Anakhane
    Raw material: White vein quartz.
    Tool type: Core.
    Description: Almost oval in shape. Shallow blade flake removed from dorsal. Uneven ventral side. Measurements 3.8 × 2.6 × 1.5 cm.
61. Site: Anakhane
    Raw material: White vein quartz.
    Tool type: Core.
    Description: Amorphous in shape. A medium size flake removed on the dorsal. Scars and ripples on the flatish ventral side. Measurements 2.5 × 1.9 × 0.7 cm
62. Site: Anakhane
    Raw material: White vein quartz.
    Tool type: Point.
    Description: Roughly triangular in shape. Fluting on the dorsal. A shallow flake detached near the working end on the left margin makes it concave. Straight right margin. Measurements 1.4 × 1.1 × 0.3 cm
63. Site: Anakhane
    Raw material: White vein quartz.
    Tool type: Point.
    Description: On roughly triangular flake. Shallow flake scars on the dorsal side. Plain ventral side. Curved straight margin. Tip retouched. Measurements 2.8 × 1.5 × 0.6 cm.
64. Site: Anakhane
    Raw material: White vein quartz.
    Tool type: Point
    Description: On roughly triangular flake. Four flutings on the dorsal. Notched on the left margin.

Pointed tip. Measurements 2.4 × 2.0 × 0.8 cm.

65. Site: Anakhane

Raw material: White vein quartz.

Tool type: Flake

Description: Roughly square. Flat dorsal and ventral sides with numerous scars. Measurements 2.4 × 1.8 × 0.5 cm.

66. Site: Anakhane

Raw material: White vein quartz.

Tool type: Flake

Description: Roughly rectangular. Flat dorsal and ventral sides with numerous scars and ripples. Measurements 2.6 × 1.9 × 0.8 cm.

67. Site: Anakhane

Raw material: Smoky white vein quartz.

Tool type: Flake.

Description: Triangular shaped. Three deep flakes scars on the dorsal. Pointed tip. Measurements 3.3 × 2.7 × 1.6 cm.

68. Site: Quepem

Raw material: Smoky white quartz.

Tool type: flake.

Description: Irregularly shaped. Thin flake. Shallow flake scars on both sides. Faintly retouched. Measurements 1.3 × 1.5 × 0.3 cm.

69. Site: Quepem

Raw material: White vein quartz

Tool type: Flake.

Description: Bladish flake. Four narrow flake scars on the dorsal. Slightly curved right margin. Retouched. Measurements 2.0 × 1.4 × 0.4 cm.

70. Site: Quepem

Raw material: White vein quartz.

Tool type: Point.

Description: On an elongated leaf-shaped flake. Steep flake scars on the right margin. High mid edge. Slightly diffused by removing two flakes obliquely. Bulb of percussion on the ventral side. Retouched along the margin. Beak-shaped tip. Measurements 4.1 × 2.0 × 1.1 cm.

71. Site: Quepem

Raw material: Smoky white quartz.

Tool type: Flake.

Description: Bladish flake. Irregular flake scars on the dorsal. Flattish ventral Sides. High mid ridge. Retouched. Measurements 3.0 × 1.5 × 0.7 cm.

5

NEOLITHIC AND MEGALITHIC SITES

In Goa, no Neolithic habitation site has been found so far unlike the occurence of such sites in large numbers in the adjoining Malaprabha, Ghataprabha and Krishna river valleys of Karnataka. However, a few Neolithic sites have been reported from Goa. Sundara (1969) was perhaps the first to pick up the fragment of a Neolithic object i.e, a pointed butt of a ground celt along with fluted core near Tambdisurla. In Sali's collection there was a complete Neolithic find, i.e., a triangular axe with ovaloid (personal communication from Sundara who accompanied Sali). The exact provenance of the celt is not known, as the relevant records do not mention about this. Banerjee (1974) had picked up three Neolithic celts at Arali, a site on the river Sal overlooking the sea. In the course of clearance of the underground chamber at Chicalim reported earlier by Mitterwallner, Sali recovered a Neolithic find in the debris covering the underground chamber. In Old Goa during the debris clearance work at the St. Cajetan church another Neolithic celt was found in 1984. All these neoliths are made on dyke. They are usually small in size. The sites are located all over Goa in all environmental conditions. Tambdisurla is located in the own ghat area; Chicalim and Old Goa are located in the near coastal area; and Arali is located on a place where river Sal merges into the sea.

Dhume (1985) in his book illustrated three implements; they are, "a handaxe found at Cavora, Quepem dating 6,000 B.C.; a handaxe found on a rock on the sea shore at Anjuna; a scimitar of basalt shist found at a depth of one metre while opening a trench at Thane village Satari dating circa I[st] century A.D." The first and last one are illustrated with photographs while the second one is illustrated with a sketch. The thickness, form and strokes in fashioning the handle, and the point are not described. Likewise, whether they bear a ground mark is not known. The tools are not available for examination. They no doubt look like cutting tools or hoes (?). During the present study, the survey carried out in the above mentioned localities was not fruitful. Even the date suggested by Dhume was not based on scientific method. At present, therefore, the tools reported by him cannot be seriously considered.

During the course of the present study, a medium-sized thin flake of dolerite dyke was found at Sancorda in Sanguem, 18 km west of Tambdisurla. It is just a thin flake without any secondary flaking. It is quite possible that this flake is the result of primary flaking of a suitable lump of dolerite dyke ultimately to shape a Neolithic celt. If this inference on this solitary flake so far found is correct, it may indicate the existence of a Neolithic factory site nearby. It may be recalled here a butt end of a Neolithic stone axe was found at a small distance from Tambdisurla.

From the above perusal it appears that the present Mandovi-Zuari basin was the focal point of Neolithic phase and Anmod on the border between Goa and Karnataka is actually a ghat highway, which has also yielded a Neolithic axe on basalt. Further eastward located is the Malaprabha valley with many Chalcolithic sites. It is quite likely that Anmod-Tambdisurla gap was used for movement between the down ghat and upghat area from the Neolithic times, if not earlier. Further fieldwork may bring to light a few more such highwa,s connecting Goa with Karnataka and even Maharashtra.

In the downghat and coastal plain south of river Mandovi upto Kerala have been reported from a few sites, for example in the Sita valley of Dakshina Kanara district of Karnataka (Sundara 1991,46-47) and near Edakkal of Kerala. (I.A, 1901,Vol XXX). Shetty (1990) collected Neolithic celts from Kotatattu, Bhandimatha, Haradi, and Nadaru all in Dakshina Kannara district of Karnataka. Almost all of them are stray finds on plain land without any Neolithic cultural debris. But in Chitari burnished grey ware sherd with red ochre painting at the edge was found. At Fatorpa, in Goa, solitary grey ware sherd was found near a megalithic stone circle during the present survey. Both of them may belong to the Neolithic/Chalcolithic phase. The fluted core made on Chalcedony found in Tambdisurla as mentioned above appears to be more of Chalcolithic contact. The solitary potsherd from Fatorpa referred to above may also belong to this phase. They may be survivals, for nowhere has any regular habitation site of Neolithic culture been reported so far.

The sporadic occurrence of Neolithic celts with meagre potsherds seems to indicate that they are the survival of the Neolithic culture overlapping with the Iron Age Megalithic phase. In fact one or two Megaliths at Hegdehalli and Koppa in North Karnataka and Coimbatore region have yielded Neolithic potsherds. The Iron Age technology and tool types seem to have wiped out the Neolithic tool type. This explains for their rare occurrence.

Shirodkar (1985) has reported quite a few Megalithic sites in Goa, which include dolmens, menhirs, stone circles, etc. Of these, the stone circles at Curdi and Bambolim are definitely of the Megalithic period. The so-called dolmens appear to be load-rests and are discussed in appendix-I. Subterranean chambers are found in Chicalim (Taluk Salcette), Neura (Taluk Tiswadi), Aldona and Tivim (Taluk Bardez). Shirodkar first noticed the Megalithic stone circles in Curdi in 1982. But prior to this the discovery of the underground chambers were reported as early as 1936 (Pissurlenker: 1936). The clearance work in one of the chambers yielded a Neolithic celt, a few grey ware sherds and an iron hook. Sali, who investigated the site in view of the occurrence of the Neolithic felt that the chambers might be of Neolithic period (A.S.I. records). Two sites, stone circles in Fatorpa and Ibrahimpur and an underground chamber at Neura were noticed in course of the present research.

Stone circles are found in Curdi, Fatorpa, Ibrahimpur and Bambolim. But the number of circles is meagre ranging from 1 to 5. The diameter of the circles varies from 6 to 11 m. The material used for boulders is laterite. For the menhirs chloritic schist is used as at Fatorpa. The boulders of the circles are not systematically juxtaposed. A few stones in the circles are not found. It is rather difficult to make out the circle particularly at Ibrahimpur. The Bambolim stone circle is in a fully disturbed condition. However, the circles in Curdi and Fatorpa are fairly regular. In none of the circles cairn packing is noticed. They are apparently similar to the cairn circle at Bramhagiri (Wheeler: 1954). Elsewhere in south India from many megalithic sites a large number of stone circles are found. The boulders in the circles are closely juxtaposed. Generally, there will be cairn packing within the circle. In consideration of these factors one doubts whether the stone circles in Goa are really sepulchral megalithic monuments.

The Goa State Archaeology opened three of the five stone circles in Curdi. In every circle quite a big quantity of red ware potsherds were found from all over the circle at different levels. There was no regular pit noticed in the circle. The depth of the excavation circles varies from .85 m to 1.5 m. A large quantity of quartz fragments was collected from the circles. Neither iron objects nor skeletal remains were found. The potteries found in the excavations are of two types, red ware and black and red ware. No whole pot was found. The Black and Red ware does not have the distinguishing polish usually found in the typical megalithic pottery from other regions. With much difficulty two or three types could be made out.

On a few sherds are found wavy lines and nail impressions. This is a rather rare feature in Megalithic pottery elsewhere but common in early historical times. The occurrence of large quantities of quartz fragments within the excavated circles is a noteworthy feature. Such feature have been reported from many megalithic sites such as Terdal and Halingalli in Jamkhandi district Bijapur, Gumchimaradi in Gokak district Belgaum, Tadakanhalli in Hirekeru district Dharwad (Sundara, personnel communication). The occurrence of Black-and-Red ware and quartz fragments indicate the Megalithic character and the absence of skeletal remains and iron objects, non-availability of full pots seem to imply that they are either primary macerating pits or dummy circles. The incised decorative patterns suggest a late date probably of the overlapping period of the Megalithic culture with early historical period, i.e, 300 B.C to Ist century A.D.

Approximately 50 m north of the Saptakoteswara temple is found a disturbed stone circle. Only three fourth of the circle is extant. There are 17 stones in the circle, varying in size from 12 × 12 cm to 55 × 12 cm. The material used for the circles is laterite and for two menhirs at the centre chlorite schist is used. What is noteworthy is the stones used for the circles are well dressed. It may be recalled that in Karnataka at Gumchimaradi and Godchimalki there are passage chamber tombs within double stone circles and one of the circles comprises of well cut and dressed rectangular laterite blocks (Sundara; 1975: 158), similar to those of the Megalithic circle at Fatorpa. Even the degree of erosion in both the sites is similar. This is an important feature, which indicates that this is a Megalithic circle. Within the circles there are two rectangular slabs fixed in a vertically inclined position, with some distance in between.

The elaborately excavated underground chambers of Kerala have been studied in detail (Sharma 1956: 93-155). They are generally found in laterite surface. Similar underground chambers are also found in coastal Karnataka (Sundara, 1991: 53-56). In Goa, underground chambers are noticed at Chicalim, Neura, Aldona, etc. The chambers are cylindrical at the top and cut to a depth of 1.5 m with .40 m diameter at the top and gradually widening to 1.20 m at the bottom. The floor is flat and even. As the entrance is narrow at the top it is difficult for one to get into the chamber. Further south in Dakshina Kanara district of coastal Karnataka and Kerala such underground chambers are found. They occur in large numbers and bigger in size, about 1 m diameter in the top and 3 m at the bottom. The chambers are found in thirteen places in coastal Karnataka such as Puttur, Perampali, Kotta, Mudanadamburu, Santuru, Belage, etc. Megalithic Black and Red ware have been reported from Santuru. The chambers are of larger dimension unlike those of Chicalim. The coastal Karnataka chambers approximately measure 1 m at the top and 3 m at the bottom and 3 m in height. They are generally pot-shaped with flat bottom and the mouth is covered with a stone slab. They also have a ramp to get in. The small chamber in Chicalim examined by Sali, has yielded one Neolithic celt and an iron hook apart from a few sherds of black-and-red ware. Similarly of plan and elevation of these chambers with those found in Kerala and Karnataka on the one hand and the occurrence of iron and black-and-red ware sherds on the other, may suggest Megalithic affiliation. They may be memorials of child burial.

On the whole, the picture of Iron Age Megalithic culture of Goa region is still dubious and very piecemeal. Surface explorations are also not very encouraging. Future research may bring to light typical megaliths from this ares. That may give a clear idea of the Megalithic culture of Goa.

In 1984, a sculpture of a female figure was found (Shirodkar, 1987; 9-15) *in situ* on a flat laterite surface about 200 mts west of the stone circle at curdi. This is a well-cut female figure (approximately measuring 2.20 mts in height, .90 mts in width and .12 mts in high relief) in supine posture, plain and simple without any garment and ornamentation except perhaps ear lobes. Even the physical feature especially of the face, stomach, fingers, etc., is not clearly marked. The figure is worn out so much so that the breasts are not so prominent. In view of the less prominent breasts, broad pelvic region and a small indistinct figure lying to the left between her chest, and hand possibly her child, it was felt that it is a female figure, probably the mother goddess. The chest, the waist, the thighs and palms are open. Actually, the laterite surface is cut into a trough leaving in the middle rock for sculpting the figure. Since the area was to be submerged under the Salauli river irrigated project, the sculpture has been carefully detached from the parent rock and transferred to Verna about 30 kms northwest of Curdi (Deshpande 1989; 78-89).

The deep cutting of the figure has exaggerated pelvis region; posture, severely plain form and indistinct facial and other features probably suggest that it may be of the Megalithic period. If this suggestion is correct then the evidence, the first of its kind of the Megalithic period, assumes more significance.

The representation of a female figure in the similar posture is found elsewhere. The posture recalls a similar depiction on a gold plaque from Lauriya Nandangarh and on terracotta from Navadatoli (Srivastava; 1979). Another example is one of the seal types of the Harappan civilization (Joshi and Parpola: 1987). Representations of anthropomorphic figure as part of the Megalithic circles or within the complex are noticed in Tamil Nadu. In Mottur (Narasimhaiah: 1980), there is an anthromorphic figure abstract in form fixed in the circle of a megalith. It was excavated and found to be of Megalithic period. In Aihole in the enclosed wall of a Megalith on rocky hilly plateau found was a more abstract anthropomorphic figure (Sundara, 1975: p.36). All these evidences, therefore, indicate that the female figure under study, near the stone circles at Curdi is also of the Megalithic context. Regarding the identification of the sculpture, Shirodkar has reasonably argued that the name of the place i.e, Curdi has something to do with this sculpture. He thinks that the name Curdi may be derived from Kotravai. Now we shall try to examine the Sangam literature. Kotravai is the Goddess of Palai of Tamil region as mentioned in Sangam literature (Sircar: 19-20). However, it may be noted here that Kotravai is not associated with a child. The reference to Kotravai in Sangam literature is quite significant for trying to understand the Curdi sculpture. She is mentioned in the Sangam literature as Vana Durga

(Srivastava: 82-3) meaning resident of forest. She is described as the presiding deity of burial grounds and living upon the dead bodies. In consideration of this reference of the sculpture in the vicinity of the Megalithic site, it is postulated that it represents a similar concept and probably a deity of Megalithic people.

The carving of sculpture in high relief may suggest that it belongs to a late phase of Megalithic culture overlapping with the historical period. The materials found in the excavated stone circles are also of late period.

Shirodkar earlier dated the sculpture to 3000 B.C. in the light of dating of Megaliths of North Karnataka to 1200 B.C. But to take into account the date of the Megaliths of North Karnataka for dating the sculpture at Curdi and by the ignoring the stone circles found in the vicinity of the sculpture looks unscientific. Hence, the suggested date needs to be reviewed. Mitragotri (1994) identified the sculpture under reference with Hariti of Buddhist affiliation in view of the depiction of a child and the discovery of Buddha sculpture at Rivona 8 kms away from Curdi and dated it to 450-500 A.D. This also may not be correct. Firstly the Buddha sculpture from Rivona is stylistically datable to 11th –12th century A.D. i.e. the Goa Kadamba period, and secondly the sculpture under reference is datable to an earlier period, on stylistic grounds as mentioned above.

APPENDIX - IV

SOME SO-CALLED MEGALITHS

(1) **Menhirs (?):** In Goa, in about 15 places, scattered all over the region, are found standing monolithic pillars of laterite, well cut square or triangular in section.

They are found in a straight line and in a group of two or three. They are of equal height and on top there may be a similar horizontal block of laterite. Usually, they are of the height of a normal human being.

Some scholars think that they are megalithic menhirs (Shirodkar). But locally they are known as *Davarnem* meaning a pillar keeping head-loads carried by the people. People carrying head-loads can keep them on the pillar and take back from that height without the help of others. Further their locations also indicate a sort of highway route. All these factors indicate that they are not Megaliths.

Stone Circle : In Kazur in front of the local temple of Paik Deva is found a circular stone enclosure. Interestingly, enough the stones of the circles are like slabs, trimmed along the edges to form a circle. They are placed one beside the other in four courses recalling the cyclopean circle of Brahmagiri. On top along the circle, slabs are placed inclining backwards as if they are back supporters of seats. It is approached through an opening in the circle, having two steps. There is a small stone enclosure comprising two slabs on the sides as high as the platform and one at the back, together looking like a shrine open to the sky. The slabs are partially dressed. On the platform two pebbles locally called *Adi Purush* and *Grampurusha* are fixed. The circle is locally believed to represent a Sabha. Shirodkar identified the circle as Megaliths. However, its location just in front of the temple, the inclined slab stones of the circle, the steps to get in and the small shrine enclosure within-all indicate that the circle is more of a religious structure of Medieval period rather than a Sepulchral or memorial Megalithic circle.

6

Rock Art

Ever since the pioneering discoveries in the last decade of this century of rock engravings at Kupgal (District Bellary, Karnataka), Edakkal (District Calicut, Kerala) by Fawcett (IA, 1901: XXX), sporadic discoveries of engravings, bruisings and paintings have been made till recently in different parts of the country. But within the last three decades comparatively there is an upsurge of discoveries especially in Karnataka and Andhra Pradesh. In this respect too, Goa did not lag behind. With the discovery of the interesting rock engravings at Usagalimol and Kazur, Taluka Sanguem on the west banks of river Kushavati in 1993, Goa now finds a place in the rock art map of India. The above-mentioned rock art specimens from the other parts of India range in date from the Mesolithic to the modern period. In Goa, some of the rock engravings particularly from Kazur are datable to the Iron Age Megalithic or to the overlapping phase of the Megalithic/Early Historical periods. Kamat (1993: 36-41) suggested a date range of 2500 B.C. to 1500 B.C. On the other hand Shirodkar (1994) opined that the engravings are of the Upper Palaeolithic/Mesolithic period and dated them to 8000 to 6000 B.C.

Located at about 20 kms south of Sanguem, the head quarters, it is in the down ghats area, with a few hills in the vicinity. The area is thickly forested which at places has been cleared for cultivation, construction activities, etc., The site is on the rain-fed stream, joining river Kushavati upstream, which is one km north of the site. Quartzite, schist, dyke, etc., are abundantly available in the form of boulders and river pebbles.

The engraved chloritic schist boulder locally called *Dhan Fator* (stone of wealth) lies about 100 mts north of Paik Nath temple in a paddy field. Local people believe that the worship of this boulder brings fortunes to them. The irregularly shaped boulder measures 1.70 mts in height and 1.90 mts in width. Only one engraved boulder was noticed in the vicinity, though similar boulders are found on the hills. On enquiry it was learnt that there were many boulders scattered in the area, but in course of time for agricultureal purposes they were removed. A terrific loss to archaeology, if some of them had similar engravings. During the survey of the area a few faint lines, probably representing a bull, were noticed on a stone slab kept in vertical position near the Paik Nath temple. The characteristic feature of the lines is similar to those of the engravings of a herd of cattle on the boulder in the field. One of the oblique lines on the orthostat extend up to the edge and seems to be continue further. If it is correct, then the slab is part of a large depiction of engravings. The orthostat is probably a remnant of boulder engravings. The engravings seem to be into some geometrical design. They recall rather vaguely the Edakkal engravings.

In the extant boulder, on the sloppy surface are carved numerous figures of bulls. Other than bulls no other animal or human beings are carved except the axe-shaped symbol at the bottom of the rock which was identified with vulva by Shirodkar. The symbol is called as *Alami* (mushroom) by the local people. All animals are shown standing facing a singular direction. There are three in the upper zone, two in the topmost, four in the middle and five in the lowest row numbering 14 in all. They are more or less similar to one another. The humps are prominent as also the virile membrane. The horns are of at least three types (a) convex a with slight bend in middle (b) 'U'- shaped with a pointed bottom and horizontally turned edges and (c) bent backwards. The 'U' shaped horn with horizontally turned edges immediately reminds one of a Harappan alphabet (Joshi & Parpola: 1987: 32,63 and 79). Similar 'U'-shaped horns are known from Gaavali (Kundapur) (Sundara 1991: 51-59).

What is interesting is that the horn of one of the bull in the lower row forms the leg of another bulls in the upper row. The engravings are deep and thick as if they are curved methodically with a metal tool. The average depth is 1 cm and width is 1.80 cm.

Similar engravings are found recently elsewhere in three places in Sonda (Sirsi, District Uttara Kannada), Holaluru (District Shimoga) all in Karnataka (Sundara, Personal communication). In both the sites, engraved on dyke boulders are bulls. In the former sites the lines of legs are drawn further downward into a knot. At Gaavali (Kundapur) District Daksina Kannada engraved (Sundara; 1991: 51) on a boulder is a bull the legs of which are carved downward into 8 knotted mandala, similar to the Navagraha mandala displayed in the religious rites of the Hindus even today. And in the vicinity of the engravings is noticed a Megalithic site. Considering the deep engravings and thick lines and the Megalithic sites nearby as well as the style and form of the animals, it is suggested that they may be of Megalithic context. Why there is an attempt at showing a knot or mandala in the above-mentioned sites in Karnataka or joining of horns and legs as at Kazur is a problem that still remains unsolved and appears to be of some significance.

The engravings on the laterite rock in the riverbed of Kushavati near Usgalimol were probably first noticed and reported by Dhume 1986,31. He says, "There were faint line carvings of an elephant and Sun on the rock" on which an axe was also found. The axe has already been discussed above. This is all that he says about the engravings. He did not seem to have realized the importance of the bruisings. Shirodkar (1993) apparently unaware of Dhume's reference reported about the engravings art Usgalimol along with the newly-found engravings at Kazur near the so-called Megaliths. Comparing with the rock bruising in Europe, Bhimbetka, etc., assigned a date of 8000-6000 B.C., i.e., Upper Palaeolithic to the Mesolithic period. In this background the engravings have been examined at both these sites and documented properly.

The engravings in Usgalimol are carved on laterite surface as mentioned earlier. The river at this place takes a sharp turn towards East exposing the laterite bed measuring approximately 60 × 60 mts on the western side. There is a gradual slope of 1.5 mts from the riverbank towards the water level. A small hillock is noticed near the vicinity where mining activity is going on at present. It is possible that soil is being washed down from the hillock rolling over the part of the engravings, over a period of time. The Directorate of Archives, Archaeology and Museum Government of Goa cleared part of the debris on the laterite bed on a trial basis and found engravings under the cover of soil. Further work in this direction may bring more engravings to light. Geomorphological study of the area specially the deposition of soil over the engraved laterite beds will help us in dating the engravings.

Coming to the archaeological aspects, there are 27 engravings noticed so far scattered all over the place. The subject included individual human beings in various

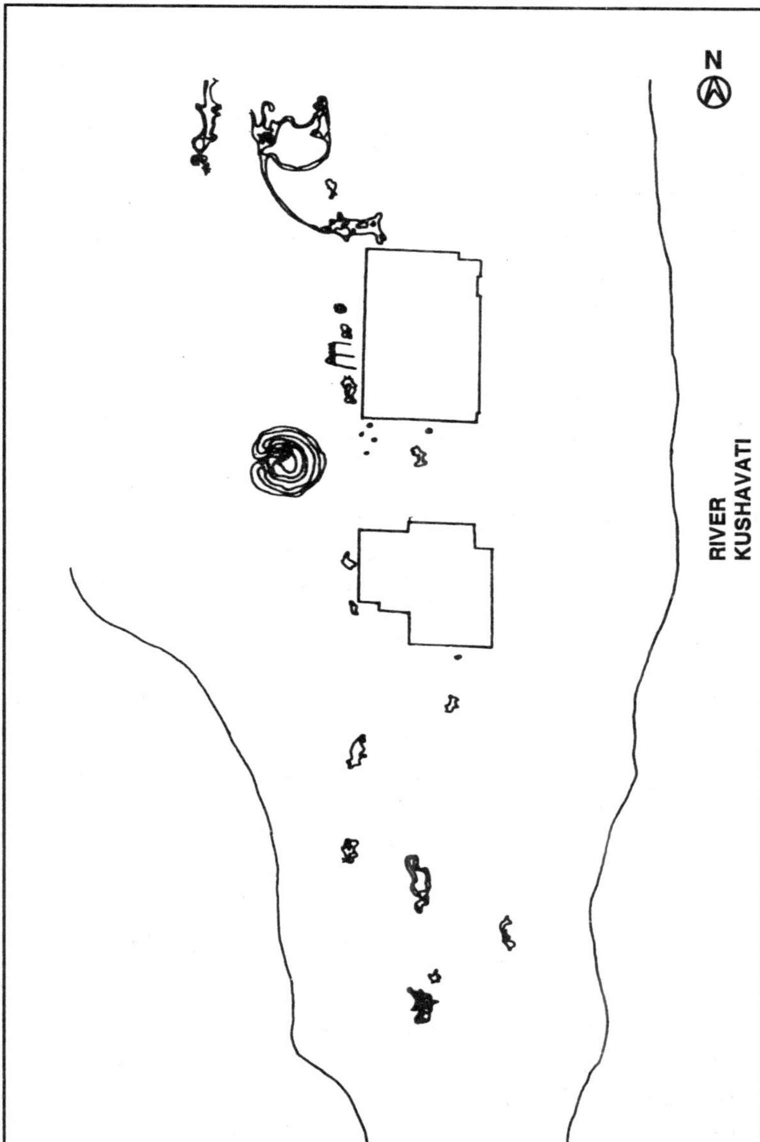

Fig. 4: Rock Engravings-Usgalimol

postures, bulls, elephants, deer, mother and child (?), footprints and more importantly the Chakradyuha. No groups are found and no orientation is followed. The width of ten engravings measures 2.00 cms and average depth is 1.50 cms. It is clear, therefore, that the brusings are wider and deeper than the ones at Kazur. The important bruisings are discussed below.

The bull depicted, as having a raised bushy tail is an interesting one as the interior lines seem to indicate the nerve system of the body. It looks as if it is an X-rayed figure. Hence, such bruisings of paintings are called X-ray figures. These types of figures are found in Bhimbetka paintings (Wakankar) in the other places. The hornes of the bulls under question are protruding forward and evenly thick. The other bull with a permanent hump has 'V' shaped horns with one of them bent forward. The elephant is not clearly engraved, however, it recalls a similar depiction in painting in Bhimbetka region.

Among the human beings, a figure is shown standing with legs stretched apart and hands raised above the horizontal line. The figure seems to sport some decorative helmet on the head. Whether it is a male or a female is difficult to identify. Another figure is shown standing on one leg while the other is bent and kept on the other leg and the hands are stretched obliquely.

Among the geometrical designs comprising concentric circles of as many as seven is noteworthy. Its winding path leads to the centre. Shirodkar identified it as triskelion. He also posted a question weather it represents the Sun symbol to calculate time. But it is more likely a Chakravyuha, a popular design even today. It is interesting to note that similar designs were found at Tikla Paintings near Gwalior, Madhya Pradesh (Wanke; 1977; 36 and 95). Three-spiral patterns joined together is noticed in a passage grave at New Grange in Ireland and are dated to 3000 B.C. (Myers & Copplestone 1993:12). Similar concentric circles are found on a stone model of a multiple grannery from Melos, Greece, dated 2500-2200 BC. (Pedley,1992; 40-41). Both these patterns closely resemble the Chakravyuha design under study. The paintings in the above-mentioned places is dated to the Mesolithic period i.e. 6000-3000 B.C. More interestingly, at Volcamonica in Italy, there in that design two foot-soldiers holding sword and shield are also shown clearly suggesting it is a rare design of the ancient times. Also the design appears to be universal.

In the Mahabharata time during the war Dronacharya Commander-in-Chief of the army of Kauravas the is said to have arranged his army according to the Chakravyuha plan (Drona Parva). It was impenetrable but Abhimanyu the most valous and courageous fighter fearlessly entered in, fought gallantly and met heroic death. The Chakravyuha design engraved in Usgalimol is now fully exposed. This design looks as though it is the actual picture design of the concept. The material that covered the engravings was disintegrated compact laterite soil probably brought down by monsoon rain on accounts of the slop as mentioned above. This really is suggestive of the antiquity of the design in particular and the engravings in general. It most probably belongs to the protohistoric period. In view of the thick and deep engraved lines it is suggested that this may be of the Megalithic period. If it is early, this may be of, the overlapping Megalithic with Chalcolithic phase. Therefore, the engravings may be dated to 1500 to 800 B.C. Most of the animal figures may also be dated to the same period.

Now, with regard to the human figures standing on one leg with outstretched hands, one is inclined to think that it may be of the historical period. Generally, human beings in such a posture are generally found in paintings and engraving of the historical period. But it may be noted that the human figure in a similar posture in the painting of Iron age Megalithic period datable to 800 to 200 B.C. are found at Sugriva Guha in Hampi area.

However, the examination of the river section at Usgalimol overlying the engravings might prove to be helpful in deciding the age more accurately. The discovery of the engraving is not only significant but also informative regarding the protohistoric culture of Goa.

Further exploration by J.V.P Rao (Personal Communication) led to discovery of engravings and bruises in Mauxi (Volpoi Taluk) about 40 km north of Panaji on the banks of river Nanora that independently joins the sea. The figures are found on basalt rock boulders like those of Kazur. During the rainy season these figures are submerged. The figures may be classified into two categories, namely, pecking and engravings.

The figures are a trisula and three cattle in isolation. The trisula is pecked, while the cattle are engraved. It is for the first time that the pecked figures are found in the region. The animals are again classifield into two kinds, namely, Bull (2 nos) and the other animal is to be identified. The characteristic horns and the prominent hump of the bulls are stylistically different from those of the bulls of Kazur. The male organ of the animal is not depicted. Further, the way the tail and the horn are shown seem to imply that these engravings are earliar than those from Kazur. The other animal, looking like a dog but for the horns and long neck is in front of a trisula. The stake of the trisula at the bottom end is bent at right angle. The style of the trisula recalls the iron trisula found occasionally in Megalithic sites from South

India. Therefore, the animals and the trisula may be of the Megalithic phase, probably datable to c. 1000 B.C.

Recently, the State Department of Archives and Archaeology and Museum has located a rock art site at Pansalimol, in the same region. Engravings found here are an animal, perhaps a bull, and three humans roughly in a row. Comparatively in the case of the bull the trifurcated bushy part of the male organ, the humps are comparable to those from Usgalimol. Even the human figurines too are stylistically similar to those from Usgalimol.

Thus, the Goa region appears to be quite promising in the rock art tradition since the sites are found in different geographical environments and covering the major part of the Goa region. Further, particularly with regard to the site at Usgalimol the discovery of the animal fossil bones about 20 kms. downwards in Kushavati valley seems to be significant. Badam has identified the fossil remains as those of Bos remidius datable to 6000 B.C. If the depiction of the Usgalimol animals are those of the fossil remains which are referred to above, then the engravings may be dated to more or less to the time of the fossil i.e. 6000 B.C. However, this is only a provisional observation. For how long such animals continue to be present in the region and in which phase of this existence the animal is indicated are not known.

A team of Scientists from the National Institute of Oceanography, Donapaula, Goa (Personal Communication) which examined the rock art sites at Kazur and Usgalimol raised a couple of questions. The engravings are done on the laterite bed. The river swells during the monsoon and covers the engravings for most part of the rainy season. Surprisingly the engravings are not eroded, and well preserved. Particularly considering the fact that Early Holocene (9000 BP) is characterised by hot and dry to hot and wet climate, marked by heavy rains along the west coast, leading to heavy terrestrial discharge. Obviously, therefore the river must have occupied a wider area. Surprisingly enough, the engravings are intact.

Based on the palynological/geological evidences Caratini (1994) suggested that in around 3000 B.C. there was a significant climatic change along the west coast of India, from humid to somewhat arid conditions.

APPENDIX - V

IMPORTANT ROCK-ART SITES IN THE WEST COAST KARNATAKA

P=Painting BR=Bruising EN=Engraving

No.	Locality	District	Nature of Rock-art
1	Hire Benkal	Raichur	P
2	Chikrampur	Raichur	P
3	Anegondi	Raichur	P
4	Tawargere	Raichur	BR
5	Mallapur	Raichur	P
6	Piklihal	Raichur	P, BR, EN
7	Billamrayangudda	Raichur	BR
8	Chik Hesrur	Raichur	BR
9	Kotekal	Raichur	BR
10	Kallur	Raichur	EN
11	Togalgudda	Raichur	P
12	Kupgal	Bellary	EN
13	Tekkalakota	Bellary	P, BR
14	Venkatapur	Bellary	P
15	Mallur	Gulbarga	BR
16	Kupgal	Gulbarga	BR
17	Hebbal Buzurg	Gulbarga	BR
18	Kodekal	Gulbarga	BR
19	Hunsgi	Gulbarga	BR
20	Bahairapur	Gulbarga	BR
21	Kodemathi	Gulbarga	BR
22	Chikanhalli	Gulbarga	BR
23	Balchakra	Gulbarga	P
24	Badami	Bijapur	P

No.	Locality	District	Nature of Rock-art
25	Shidlaphadi	Bijapur	P
26	Totkoti	Bijapur	P
27	Sitidoni hill	Bijapur	P
28	Mahakut	Bijapur	P
29	Kullolli	Bijapur	EN
30	Bhole	U. Kannada	EN
31	Angola	U. Kannada	EN
32	Sonda	U. Kannada	EN
33	Holaluru	Shimoga	EN
34	Gaavali	D. Kannada	EN

APPENDIX – VI

ROCK-ART SITES IN KERALA

No.	Locality	District	Nature of Rock-Art
1	Edakkal	Kozhikode	EN
2	Tenmalai	Quilon	EN
3	Maraiyur	Kottayam	P

7

Early Historical Period

The term early history used here denotes the periods of the Mauryas, the Satavahana, the Gupta, the early Chalukya, the early Pallava and the early Kadambas of other areas. The occurrence of a lone fragmentary edict of Asoka, the Mauryan emperor, in Sopara is well known. The southern-most Asokan edict is the one found at Brahmagiri. This can be taken as the southern-most part of the Asokan Empire known so far. The Goa region on the west coast falls within the latitudes of Sopara and Brahmagiri. It is possible that within the Mauryan empire Goa was also included. If this surmise is correct then this is the earliest evidence of Goa region being in the early historical period.

Evidences shedding light on the early historical period of the region under study are few and far between. Even these evidences are either fragmentary or not so informative. Apart from the traditional account referred to in chapter I, the direct palpable evidences are the literary references to the names of the region in the Periplus and Ptolemy's Geography of the Ist and 2nd century A.D. respectively. So far as archaeological evidences are concerned the Shiroda copper plate of Devaraja (EI XXX, 1932 pp, 143-65), the two early Kadamba inscriptions from the Arvalem caves and the fragmentary Kannada inscription from Chandor are noteworthy. Preliminary digging carried out in 1974 by S.R. Rao at the Siva temple in the Kota (fort) area of Chandor revealed two phases of structural activity; the earlier one representing the Satavahanas and the later, the Kadambas. Besides this evidence, the Aravelam, a rock-cut cave, is located which may be dated to 5th-6th century A.D. In the course of present field work a small rock-cut cell enshrining a seated lion on a pedestal carve *in situ* was discovered. This is indeed an important discovery.

Regarding the trade and commercial activity of the Goa region during the early historical period Gune (1979) mentioned that in Mapusa red ware sherds resembling Roman cups, a few sherds of rouletted ware and two coins were found in the Brahma Varta area. However, he neither illustrated nor gave a detailed account of the objects found.

Buddha sculpture from Colvale a Bardez (Heras; 1980; 73-86) is an important find. The earlier scholars dated it to 2nd century A.D. It appears to be of a slightly later period than what was suggested. These points will be discussed in this chapter. Thus, the evidence now available would not help much to reconstruct the culture of the region during the early historical period. However, an attempt has been made to define the available material as much as possible.

Goa is also referred to as Gopakavana and Gopakapattana. With regard to the three variable Gopaka vana, Gopaka pura and Gopattana. It is interesting to note there are a few other regions having the same name with varying suffixes such as Vana pura and Pattana. For example Chitradurga (district headquarter in Karnataka) near Chandravalli archaeologically well known in the Cholcolithic stage, the Iron Age (Megalithic) and the early historical period, is referred to as Idumba vana, Idumba Grama and Idumba Pattana. It is all the more interesting to note that these names, found in the rise of 12th to 14th century A.D. seem to indicate as if the three stages of cultural process the Neolithic, a village in a forest associated with Idumba Asura demon hero of the Mahabharata war; the Iron Age megalithic town and the early historical city. Whether a similar cultural situation is indicated in the Goa region needs to be investigated. Govarashtra is one of the divisions of Parasurama Kshetra. Lord Krishna, enchanted by the beauty of the land and Gopikas named it Goparashtra. The Padma Purana refers to the country of Gomanta wherein is located the mountain called Gomantagiri. Narivamsa also mentions this mountain where Krishna and Balarama defeated Jarasanda. However Harivamsa locates the mountain in Uttara Kannada district.

With regard to the Jarasanda legend it may be noted that his kingdom is located in Bihar. Jarasanda fought Bhima and Krishna. Therefore it is to be verified whether there is any hill called Gomachala in Bihar. It is therefore likely that the Gomanchala of Harivamsa purana may not be Goa region. However, in the wake of the spread of the Krishna and Pandava legend, it is quite likely that the inheritors of the traditions might have named the new settlements with the old names of their home. And in that case Goa could be the Gomanchala of Harivamsa indicating it to be the settlement of the inheritors.

The Saurashtra region is known to have been rich in the Harappa cultural sites. In the wake of the decline of the Harappa civilization there were series of cultural diffusion and it appears from the nucleus region towards Deccan also. One such diffusion and might have been along the west coast. This may explain the subsequent naming of the region as Gomantaka after the original name in Saurashtra by the incoming people of Harappan civilization.

Other names with which Goa is associated are Shurparaka desa. It may be noted here that scholars are in agreement as to the identification of Shurparaka with the present Sopara. Here, a fragment of the Asokan Edict has been found and the Goa region might have been included in the Shurparaka desa. It indicates that Goa was quite active and well developed around 4th century B.C. so as to be referred to as Shurparaka desa. There is another area located in the Uttara Kannada district of Karnataka known as Supa. According to the local legend Supa was derived from Shrupa, meaning, a winnow. In fact the Supa valley looks like a winnow. But no archaeological remains have so far been reported. But in the recent years within a reasonable distance from Supa in a village called Anmod, a Neolithic celt has been found. That is to say that during the Neolithic times or slightly later this area seemed to have been culturally active. This Supa area is actually bordering on the Goa region. A thorough investigation is therefore necessary in Supa area to trace the cultural remains, if there be any.

The Sahayadri Khanda of Skanda Purana (pt-II, ch.1) refers to the reclamation of part of Goa from the sea by Parasurama the sage, also the 6th incarnation of Lord Vishnu. It is mentioned that Parasurama performed the asvamedha yajna at Harmal (modern Arambol, Pernem). After offering all the lands he conquered, to Kashyapa, he shot seven arrows from Sahayadri (Ulhas says it was from Chandraparvat: 1994) towards the sea and reclaimed the land of trapezoid shape extending from Vaitarni to Kanyakumari. The region thus exposed goes by the name Parasurama kshetra. It is divided into 8 divisions known as Sapta Konkan. They are Viratam, Karatam, Barbara, Konkanam, Govarashtra, Tulangum,

Keralam and Havyagam. Govarashtra is Goa and the place where the arrow fell is believed to be Banauli (modern Benaulim, Salcette). The legend further states that Parasurama brought 96 Brahmins from Tirhut and settled them at Tiswadi (Tis-thirty, wadi-village) and Sashti or Salcette (66 villages).

With regard to the extent to which Parasurama threw his axe or arrow and the place from where he threw the information may vary from region to region. In Uttara Kannada the legend states that Parasurama stood from Gokarna and shot the arrows southwards. Therefore, the entire coastal belt goes by the name Parasuramakshetra excluding Gokarna and the region north of it. In Thirthahalli (Shimoga district) region the locals state that Parasurama stood on Sahyadri in Tirthahalli and threw the axe. It is also believed that Parasurama enshrined a linga at this place. There is a rock in this village supposed to have been broken by Parasurama with his axe. It is to be noted that in both the above- mentioned cases Goa is excluded.

Interestingly Parasurama legend prevails in the Malwan region of North Goa. According to the legend Parasurama shot an arrow southwards from Parasurama hill in Pedhe near Sangameswar, district Ratnagiri, and reclaimed the land (1962; Ratnagiri Gazetteer). As per this version Goa is included in the Parasuramakshetra. It is to be noted here that Sahyadri Khanda of the Skanda Purana also refers to Sangameswar as Parasuramakshetra or Ramakshetra and mentions a temple built by Parasurama himself. According to another legend prevailing in Chiplun area, Parasurama shot the arrow from Sahyadri Mountain on the Krishna River and the ocean retreated 18 coss (36 miles). In Goa people believe that Parasurama shot the arrow from Sahyadri and the arrow fell at Benauli, Salcette. There was a temple of Parasurama called Sankheswar and

Baneswar at Benaulim. The Portuguese destroyed the temple during 16th century A.D. (Pereira 1978:86). All these indicate the spread of the Parasurama cult by the inheritors of the legend. Thus, Goa is not included in the Parasuramakshetra as per the version prevailing Gokarna region. It is perhaps because the legend existing in Malwan region and Goa. On the whole the discussion on the etymology, its variants and legends seem to imply that Goa region has an interesting cultural past.

Thus, the traditions recounted in detail above, associate the Goa region with the activities of the Mahabharata period. Based on this tradition in the history of Goa could be pushed back slightly to an earlier period i.e, pre Mauryan.

In Chandrapur proper there is a brick temple locally called *Isvarache Bhat* (Place of Lord Siva). It appears from the study of Father Heras' work that the temple may belong to the early Kadamba period (1932: 14-17). Rao of the Archaeological Survey of India examined the site in 1974. He also carried out the trial digging near the temple. But his observation are unpublished, however, the perusal of the relevant record of the Archaeological Survey of India was made possible by the authorities. A reading of the records in the light of the excavator's opinion indicates two structural periods at the temple. 1. Satavahana 2. Early Kadamba.

Rao observed the existence of the earlier structure under the Kadamba temple. His opinion is based on the size of the brick and the stratigraphy. This is further substantiated by the occurrence of 29 Satavahana copper coins, a few copper nails and a few red ware sherds in the lower level. The excavated objects are in the collection of the Archaeological Museum, Velha Goa. The coins are heavily corroded and details are worn out, hence they could not be studied properly. Therefore, whether the coins belong to the Satavahana period or not could not be ascertained. However, their weight and chemical composition if ascertained may help in determining the date in comparison with similar coins from other Satavahana site. The other copper objects cannot be dated to the Satavahana period in the absence of other datable material from this level. The study of potsherds indicated that except one black ware sherd others belong to the medieval period and not to the Satavahana period.

It appears that by about 5th century A.D. Chandrapura was a prosperous city of a kingdom, for the earliest copper plate inscription from this region was found at Shiroda in the course of a casual excavation there. It speaks of one Devaraja, apparently ruling from *Sri Vijaya Chandrapura*. It indicates the place as probably the capital of a small kingdom. Unfortunately, except in the name of the royal family, no other detail about the king is available. The family was known by the name Gomin that perhaps may be connected with *Gomayana* (Gotra). Further the record makes reference to a division in the kingdom and the name of the village. The division is *Jiyaya* and the village is *Thanniyarka-Kottinkayya*.

The Archaeological Survey of India carried out excavations at Chandor during 2001-03 in the temple site and also in the fort area (Personal Communication; J.V.P. Rao & Kalimuthu). The excavations brought to light a laterite stonewall and a broad stone enclosure wall for the temple complex.Trenches laid at the *Devantolai* (temple tank), Kolamb Dhamatari and Chola areas of Chandor yielded a series of rammed floors with laterite granules and tile packing. A burnt floor was also unearthed which was probably the result of constant burning activity. Trenches laid in the Rarura area yielded imported glazed pottery, indicating trade activity.

Pissurlenkar (*op. cit.*), the archaeologist of the Portuguese Government of Goa in 1933, studied the copper plate on the basis of the transliteration provided by Krishmacharulu (EI XXIV), who edited the text. Pissurlenkar tried to identify the *Jiyaya* with some local territorial division perhaps Salcette. Further he identified *Thanniyarka-Kottinkayya* with Thanem-Kuttal in Salcette. It is rather difficult to accept the identification of *Jiyaya* with Salcette, because the derivation of the latter from the former is not satisfactory. The only way perhaps is to find out the names of the places prior to their undergoing changes during the Portuguese region. Regarding the identification of *Thanniyarka-Kottinkayya* with Thanem-Kuttal in Salcette may probably be correct, for this place is located above 30 km north of Chandrapura. Kuttal may be a sub division of the village Thane.

There is also a reference in the plates to *Prabhunaga-Bhogikamatya*, who probably made the grant ratified by his overlord Devaraja. It indicates one of the designations of ministers namely *Boghikamatyah* under the king. He was also called the Prabhu, obviously he was in charge of a division of the kingdom.

Besides two more designations of officials of administration are known. They are *Sarvatantradhikritah* (Superintendent of all departments) and *Rahasyadhikritah* (private Secretary). Amareswara who executed a grant was occupying the former office while Prabhakara who also composed the text, occupied the latter office.

The cultural importance of the period may be inferred from the record. It speaks of a grant of land probably by Prabhunaga Bhogikamatya to two Brahmins, Govindaswamin and Indraswamin of Bharadwaja Gotra. The grant includes a grihasthana (house site), goprachara (pastoral land for cows) and certain taxes from Thaniyarhaka village. The taxes were on the merchandise brought into the village. The grant further enjoins the supply of *trina* (grass) and *Kasta* (fuel wood) to the donees. The record is dated i.e, 12th regnal year of the king, on the Dwadashi (12th day) of the Krishnapaksha (dark fortnight) in the month of Magha. The exact date cannot be ascertained. However, on palaeographical grounds the inscription may belong to circa 4th century A.D.

The identity of Devaraja is so far not established, for he is not known from any other inscription. What is more interesting is the name of the royal family Gomin. As mentioned above the region was known as Gomantaka in the Mahabharata. Whether there is any connection between Gomin and Gomantaka is to be thoroughly examined although there is partial similarity between the two and thus the reference is important. Since the copper plate ends with the expression *svasty - astu dharaska – vacaka – Srotribhya* iti - and it is composed in chaste Sanskrit, it is quite likely that Devaraja was a Brahmin and followed the Vedic traditions.

Ministers and many officials assisted the king. One of the ministers was *Bhogi–Kamatya* and officials were *Sarvatantradhikritah* and *Rahasyadhikritah*. The kingdom was comprised of many divisions and *Jiyaya* was one of them. The ministers were given some land and wealth as renumeration for their services. They were therefore called *Prabhu Naga Bhogikamatya*. They were looking after the internal administration of the area under them. The *Sarvatantradhikritah* was the officer who implemented the royal orders and the *Rahasyadhikritah* maintained the important office records. Already Manusmriti and other texts were well known and used as an authority in the administration as known from the imprecatory verses of the record. As elsewhere the *Srotribya* Brahmanas occupied a high place in the society as implied in the last sentence of the record as mentioned above.

Thus, we get some interesting insight into the facets though very fragmentary of the society during the 4th century A.D. in the Goa region.

The other two records from Arvalem are palaeographically dated to 5th century A.D. They comprise of box-headed characters and very much similar to those of the early Kadamba inscriptions from Banavasi and Kundnapura (Gopal 1985). The one-line inscriptions are found on one of the horizontal pattika of a peculiar form of linga, housed in cell number two at Arvalem. The inscription reads *Sambaluru Vasi Ravih,* meaning Ravi the resident of Sambaluru. He was probably responsible for enshrining the linga there. The other inscription was noticed in cell no.1 written on the square lower part of the linga. It was a pillar with inscription, forming part of a temple. Probably, when the Portuguese destroyed the temple, the pillar was carved into the shape of a linga. Sundara who examined the linga recently opined that it was a case of a pillar linga, which is of course broken. Hence the inscription written on it is incomplete. The inscription is datable to 5th century A.D. on palaeographical grounds. The inscription also refers to Mrigasaraman, which also supports the suggested date of the cave (Gopal: 1985: 175-77).

According to the first view that it was a pillar converted into a linga, so the date of the linga will be later than the pillar inscription. According to the second view, the linga is contemporaneous with the inscription. Gopal suggested that the inscription was written first by keeping the pillar horizontally and it was placed in its position vertically. The method followed here is very similar to the one used in writing the Kudnapura and Talagunda inscriptions.

The linga, tapering in profile with a pointed top and has the Brahmasutra flowing from an arrow mark suggest a date of 4th-5th century A.D. for the sculpture. Thus, iconographically too, it is contemporaneous with the inscription, according to Sundara's observation (personal communication).

Interestingly, the inscription refers to Mahalaya to the south and also to ascetics practising Yoga and meditation. The temple appears to have been situated in a thick forest as the inscription says "God Siva is visible in a garden-like forest". The inscription refers to a Mahadeva temple in the midst of a scenic forest and also Mrigesavarman, indirectly. Whether Mrigesavarman was responsible for the temple construction, it is not clear as the lower part of the linga on which the inscription is written is broken and hence the inscription is fragmentary. It is obvious from the text that the linga was originally in the temple and subsequently brought and enshrined here. The reason for this is not known. Further there are four more cells in the cave, in three of which installed are lingas of distinct types. One of them resembles the above-mentioned linga. The other two are of a peculiar form. One looks like a spear with attenuated waist at the bottom and the other carrying a disc-like top on the shaft irregularly hexagonal in section.

The one-line inscription is written on this linga on the pattika between the shaft and the pillar. Sundararajan is of the opinion that this linga represents *Shadayatana* order. And the spear-like linga and the one with the disc like top represent respectively Karthikeya and Surya. Sundara on the other hand thinks that the peculiarly designed lingas were originally *Yupa Stambhas* connected with the Vedic sacrifices as they conform to a general prescription of *Yupa Stambhas*. Such Yupas symbolise Siva. When other Siva lingas were being enshrined, these Yupas were also included in them, he suggested. Indirectly, these will indicate that the origin of the linga form can be traced to the Vedic sacrifices.

The Chandrapura fragmentary stone inscription is in the possession of the local landlady Mrs. Sara Fernandes. Shirodkar (1983:142 and IAR 1983-84:166) made a passing reference to the inscription earlier, however the importance of the inscription is not realized. The record has not so far been studied in detail. Palaeographically, it can be dated to 6th-7th century A.D. As the language is in Kannada and the script is in a developmental stage from Brahmi to Kannada, the record is very important. Therefore, it is a milestone in tracing the development of the script in this region. Further, it also indicates the Kannada language and script was prevalent in Goa even as early as 6th-7th century A.D., as in Karnataka.

Only the imprecatory portion of the inscription is extant. Interestingly, the record mentions the name of the sculpture Desaloja, who engraved it. We may infer from this that the practice of persons bearing Kannada names was in vogue, at the same time it might have been noted that sculptors and architects might have come from outside and therefore it need not be taken as belonging to the concerned region. Anyway, the inscription helps us in dating the antiquity of the Kannada language and script in Goa region 6th-7th century A.D.

The seated image of the Buddha from Colvale, Bardez, is quite significant, for it was the first Buddhist relic ever found in Goa (Heras: 1980,73-86). The image broken in three pieces is now in the collection of the Heras the Institute of Indian History and Culture, Bombay. The Buddha is seated in Siddhasana, the hands are in Dyanamudra. The Usnisa is clearly shown. The hair is curly, the eyes are closed and the face is serene. The nose is flattish and lips are thick, the chest is broad. He is wearing Sanghati over his left shoulder. The folding of the garment is broad. On stylistic grounds, the sculpture is dated to the late first century A.D. by Heras.

However, from a thorough examination of the image it is suggested that it may belong to 4th-5th century A.D. and not to the date suggested by Heras. For the oval-shaped nimbus, the sharp lines in the neck region and the rather slender body, the mode of resting toes on the right leg on the left and the ardhoraka are typical of the 4th-5th century A.D. Interestingly, enough the Uttariya has rich folds and the lines of folds are very sharp. Similar sculptures are found in Bhaprawada, near Ankola (Uttara Kannada district), Aihole (Bijapur district) and a few places in Kerala (Amma. 1993). This sculpture is very similar in particular to the Buddha images from Aihole and Kerala. In the sculpture at Baprawada, the Uttariya is just indicated by a sharp line without any folds. The sculpture therefore in comparison with the above mentioned sculptures might be dated 4th-5th century A.D., especially in view of the wide and prominent eyes and broad chest reminiscent of similar sculptural forms of the early historical period.

The newly discovered a rock cut cell in Shigao is located just on the bank of the river. The cell square in plan measures 2.10 × 2.05 m with a maximum height of 1.34m. The cave has no decoration excepting a pilaster on either side of the entrance. A couchant lion is carved on a pedestal against the rear wall of the cell. Its back is attached to the wall. Only the outline of the face and the main is carved. The front legs are half sculptured indicating that the sculpture is incomplete.

There are two interesting aspects with regard to the sculptures of the region. The lion sculpture from Shigao and the Buddha image from Convale are of utmost importance. With regard to the lion, the northwestern part of Karnataka has produced quite a few sculptures of Dvibhuja Narasimha. Sundara who found these sculptures, after detailed study of these sculptures and also those from Goa the suggested three stages of development of the iconography of Narasimha. One of the incarnations was completely represented in the lion-like zoomorphic form of Varaha incarnation, as found at Eran (Madhya Pradesh). The sculpture from Neura and Shigao in Goa region and Kodlu Magaravalli (Tirthahalli, Shimoga District) also represent the early phase. Dvibhuja Narasimha sculpture represents the next phase and finally Chaturbhuja Narasimha images were developed with elaborate carvings.

There were two shrines of Narasimha located at Dauji in Tiswadi and Sancoale in Salcette. They were obviously of the medieval period. The Portuguese, destroyed both the temples. (Pereira 1978: 46 and 107). However, no tradition exists in the above villages with regard to Narasimha worship. Mitragotri (1993:131-32) suggested that the worship of Narasimha was brought to Goa during the Kadamba period. But the discovery of the lion sculpture at Shigao pushes back the Narasimha worship to a much earlier date.

The Shigao sculpture may go back to even 4th century A.D. It is interesting to note here that the cave is very small, looking like a cavern in which lions are supposed to be resting. This also indicates an early date for the sculpture. For tracing the north-south iconography these evidences are very important. The Buddha image in Colvale resembles the sculptures from the Kerala region. However, they are different in style from that of the Baprawada image, which is located in between the two above-mentioned regions.

Stylistically, the Buddha image from Colvale may be placed along with the Buddha sculpture from Kerala. The suggested date is 4th century A.D. On the whole the early historical remains of Goa do not give a continuous outline of a comprehensible picture of the life and society of the early historical period. The discussion looks like critical notes on various fragmentary evidences, woven with much difficulty.

8

CONCLUSION

The region under study comprises 250 localities covering an area of 3,701 sq. km. Out of 250 localities, the fieldwork carried out covers 120 localities covering the entire region. In other words the present work has covered 50% of the region. This has given a fairly good picture of the behavioural pattern of the human settlement right from the early Palaeolithic to the early historical period ending with 6th century A.D., in so far as my study is concerned. It may be noted here that the present work was commenced in 1989. During the course of the explorations in Goa, Early Palaeolithic tools such as choppers, hand axes, etc., from Shigao area were collected. From around the same time or slightly later say from 1990, Goudllar also started exploring the southern part of Goa. He also collected hand axes, cleavers, etc., from Collem, Tambdisurla and other places. They represent the earliest discovery of Acheulian tools from Goa region. Since then a good number of sites of the early middle and Upper Palaeolithic and Mesolithic cultural phases have been noticed and studied.

It is obvious from the study of the sites discovered earlier that the early middle and Upper Palaeolithic sites are few and far between. Even the tools from the above sites are small in number. Further, a considerable part of this region forms the coastal strip. Near the ghat, the hilly land is covered with thick evergreen and semi-evergreen forests. Within this region there are two major rivers with some pockets of pebble beds.

Now, owing to the coastal region being submerged a few times between 2,00,000-50,000 years B.C., the land available during the early and Middle Palaeolithic stages has been reduced in area. Another reason for this is the tidal nature of the rivers, the backwaters of which would cover the interior land also. This may perhaps explain for the occurrence of a small number of Early and Middle Palaeolithic sites. This appears to be more possible in view of the non-occurrence of Early Palaeolithic sites in the coastal region.

The present work has brought to light a highly potential Middle Palaeolithic site at Anakhane. The site is located in the middle reaches of Talpona river and on an elevated land. The other two middle Palaeolithic sites, which were discovered earlier, are located close to the sea. This brings out the fact that the Middle Palaeolithic man was able to adapt to two entirely different environments i.e, the down ghat and the coastal. Besides, the work also showed that Shigao was probably under continuous occupation from the Early Palaeolithic to the Mesolithic times through the Middle Palaeolithic phase. The evidence for the Middle and Upper Palaeolithic phase at Shigao is meagre and the collection is from the surface. However, the material available indicates clearly this aspect. A more intensive survey and excavation in the area may throw better light on this aspect.

Equally important is the evidence for the Upper Palaeolithic from Molanguinim cave site. Mitragotri and Shirodkar noticed the cave earlier. However, the work carried out there indicated that the cave was under occupation during the Upper Palaeolithic and Mesolithic times. Here also the evidence for the Upper Palaeolithic is meagre however more reliable as it is from a trial trench.

In contrast to the Early, Middle and Upper Palaeolithic sites, the Mesolithic sites are numerous especially in the central dissected plain. Here also it may be noted that the sea level around 4000 B.C. was almost as at the present. From that time upto 500 B.C. the sea level was fluctuating between 1-6 mts.

This may explain why there is less number of Mesolithic sites in the coastal strip. On the whole the environmental conditions had a serious impact on the settlement pattern of the pre-historic man. It looks as though it was a struggle between the intruding man and the changing environment, a feature distinctive of the down ghat-coastal region. Another noteworthy point is that, unlike the adjacent Malaprabha-Ghataprabha valleys, which provide an enormous quantity of rock materials all along, in Goa region with fluctuating sea level and thick forests, the availability of suitable rock material was limited for the early Palaeolithic man. The vein quartz used by the succeeding people is fractured and coarse.

The Early, Middle and Upper Palaeolithic sites are very few in number. However, the types and techniques of manufacture are broadly similar to what was prevalent in the adjacent Malaprabha-Ghataprabha valleys of Karnataka. It may be noted here that in the north of Goa i.e, Malwan region of Ratnagiri district there are a few sites with negligible occurrence of hand axes. Especially in view of the fact that the tract between Malwan and Shigao areas has not yielded any Early Palaeolithic sites in the course of the fieldwork so far, the movement from Ratnagiri region appears to be weak.

Also no sites have been reported from Karwar area, south Goa. Therefore, it looks as though there was an intrusion of people from Karnataka across the ghats.

Goa region seems to have become active from the human cultural point of view, particularly from the Mesolithic phase i.e, 4000 B.C. onwards upto 2000/1000 B.C. This would indicate that while the Deccan and western India were having villages and towns in the Chalcolithic stage, the Goa region continued to be in the Mesolithic stage. The tool types too would indicate the same date range suggested above for the Mesolithic culture. In this phase the life-style in the coastal region and the cultural part had their own distinct features. Again with reference to the kind of foods available in the respective regions, seafood might have constituted a considerable part of the diet in the coastal region.

The Neolithic culture seems to have made its appearance very late, probably in the early part of the 1st millennium B.C. to be followed soon by the Iron Age Megalithic culture. Consequently there is hardly any evidence of considerable proportion available for understanding the life of the people in the Neolithic stage. Even the evidence of the Megalithic culture is not substantial, so far to know their lifestyle. Even the disposal of the dead which has very dintinctive features elsewhere is not clear in Goa region. But to some extent it appears it is compensated by the occurrence of rock engravings at Usgalimol and Kazur. They comparatively have their own distinct features that are characteristic of the coastal and down ghat region found at Bhole near Ankola, Gawali – all located in coastal Karnataka-Sonda, Haleluru-located in the down ghat region.

The rock engravings indicate that the people were pastoral nomads with a bias for cattle and familiar with wild animals such as elephants. Of all the representations, the Chakravyuha is quite significant in particular. It seems to have a widespread distribution. Especially in consideration of the elaborate description of an army taking position in the Chakravyuha pattern in the Mahabharata. Whether this indicates the survival of the tradition from the Mahabharata period, when its knowledge was quite popular in the army strategy, is to be investigated. It may also be noted that the intricate design was already popular probably from the Mesolithic period, if the date given to the painting from Tikla, Madhya Pradesh is acceptable. Although the tradition is rich and curious for the Goa region as known from the Mahabharata and the Puranas, unfortunately the contemporary material evidences are still not available for the proto-historic period. But in this area, further study is required to understand the significance of the legends and cultures.

However, the reference to the region by the unknown author of Periplus and Ptolemy and the references to Gomin and Gomayana in the Shiroda copper plates is an encouraging point that, around the beginning of the Christian era, the region was so popular as to find mention in the brick temple belonging to the Satavahana period and 7th century inscription from Chandor. The Buddha image from Colvale, the lingas from Arvalem, the lion sculptures from Shigao and Neura do throw sufficient light on some aspects of the mode and kind of administration, i.e., the tradition, kingship with council ministers, the prevalence of the Vedic and Puranic cultures and Buddhism are like a silver lining in the dark clouds in so far as the early historical period is concerned. In this direction also further study is needed for a better understanding of the life and culture of the people during this period.

Bibliography

Acharya, G.V. 1984. Chandella Grant of Harihara, *Epigraphia Indica* Vol.XXI, pp.17-23.

Achuthankutty, C.T. et. *al.*1979. Dry land Tidal Variations in Zooplanktonic Populations in the Zuari Estuary, *Mahasagar*, Bulletin of National Institute of Oceanography, Goa, pp.169-74.

Ahmed, E. 1972. *Coastal Geomorphology of India*, Orient Longman, New Delhi.

Amma, Padmakumari. 1993. *Jain, Buddhist Temples, Early History of Kerala*, Unpublished Ph.D Thesis, Calicut University, Kerala.

Ananda, P. *et al.* 1979. Graphic Pattern of Foramaniferal Dominance in Near shore region of Central West Coast of India, *Mahasagar*, Bulletin of National Institute of Oceanography, Goa, pp.195-99.

Agrawal, D.P. & S.Kusumgar. 1974. *Prehistoric Chronology and Carbon dating in India*, Munshiram Manoharlal, New Delhi

Agrawal, D.P., Avasia, R.K. & S.J.Guzder.1973. A multi disciplinary approach to the quaternary problems in Maharashtra, *Radio carbon and Indian Archaeology*, Bombay. pp.3-17

Bhatsoori, K.G.1990. A Neolithic Axe From Anmod - A Note, *Archaeology of Karnataka*, Directorate of Archaeology & Museums, Government of Karnataka, Mysore, pp.81-84

Caratini, C. 1994. A less humid climate since c.3500rom marine cores off Karwar, West India (Abstract), *First national Symposium on IGBP*, 1987.

Crowford, Arthur. 1987. *Legends of the Konkan*, Asian Educational Services, New Delhi.

Da Silva, Ladis., 1978. *Legendary Chandor, Seat of Kadamba Dynasty*, Panaji.

Desai, A.G. & V.V. Peshwai. 1978. Drainage Anomalies in the West coast Region of Maharashtra and Goa- A Study Based on Landsat Imagery and Aerial Photo Interpretation, *Proceedings of Symposium on Morphology and Evolution of West Coast.*

Desai, C.G., 1985. Surface Water Resources for Goa's Development, *Earth Resources for Goa's Development* (Seminar Papers).

Desai, P.B., 1965. *Goa an Integral Part of Karnataka Geographical Historical and Cultural Facts*, Director of Publication and Information, Bangalore.

Desai, S. 1976. *Goa, Daman, Diu, Dadra and Nagar Haveli*, Publication Division, New Delhi.

Deshpande, M.S. 1989. Mother Goddess – A Great Leap from Kurdi to Verna, *Purabhilekh-Puratattva*, Directorate of Archives, Archaeology and Museums, Government of Goa, Panaji, Vol.VII, pp.78-89.

De Souza, T.R. 1982. Ghat Passes and Ghat Routes in South Konkan, *Unpublished Paper Submitted in 30th Punyathi Seminar on Shivaji University,* Pune.

—. (Ed) 1989. *Essays in Goan History*, Concept Publishing Company, New Delhi.

— (Ed) 1990. *Goa Through the Ages*, Vol.I & II, New Delhi.

Dhume, A.R.S., 1985. *The Cultural History of Goa (from 10,000 BC – 1352 AD),* Panaji.

Dikshit, K.N., 1968. *The Origin and Distribution of Megaliths in India,* Unpublished paper presented in Seminar on the Problem of Megaliths in India, Varnasi.

—, (Ed). 1983. Geographic Features of West Coast of India between Bombay and Goa, *Contribution to Indian Geography*, New Delhi, pp.240-60.

Doshi, Sarayu. (Ed). 1983. *Goa-Cultural Patterns*, Marg Publications, Bombay.

Fawcet, F.1894. Notes on Rock Carvings in the Edakkal Cave, Wynad, *Indian Antiquary*, Vol. XXX. pp-409.

—, 1916. Prehistoric Rock Pictures near Bellary, *Asiatic Quarterly Review*, New Series III.

Fleet, J.F. 1870. Some Further Inscriptions Relating to Kadamba Kings of Goa, *JBBRAS*, Vol.IX, pp.263-13.

Fonseca, J. N. 1986. *Sketch of the City of Goa*, New Delhi.

Foote, R.B. 1916. The *Foote Collection of Indian Prehistoric and Protohistoric Antiquities*, Madras.

Gai, G.S. 1962. Gadivore Grant of Shastadeva II, *Epigraphia Indica*, Vol.XXXIV, pp.105-10.

Gaur, A.S.1992. Excavations at Gopakapattana, *Journal of Marine Archaeology*, Vol.3.

Gaussen, H., *et al.* 1969. *Interntional Map of Vegatation and Environmental Conditions, ICAR*, New Delhi.

Gokul, A.R. 1985. Structure and Tectonics of Goa, in *Earth resources for Goa's development,* pp.14-21, Hyderabad, GSI.

Gomes Olivinho, J.F. 1987. *Village Goa*, New Delhi.

Gopal, B.R. 1985. *Corpus of Kadamba Inscriptions*, Vol.I, Sirsi.

Goswamy, S.C., *et al.* 1979. Diel and Tidal Variations in Zooplanktonic Populations in the Zuari Estuary, *Mahasagar*, Bulletin of National Institute of Oceanography, pp.247-258.

Goudellar, D.L. & Ravi Korisettar. 1993. The First Discovery of Acheulian Bifaces in Goa – Implications for the Archaeology of the West Coast of India, *Man and Environment*, Vol.XVIII, Pune.

Govindarajan, S.V. et al. 1974. *A Survey of National Resources of Goa*, New Delhi.

Gune, V.T. (Ed). 1979. Gazetter *of the Union Territory Goa, Daman and Diu*, Part 1, Panaji.

—, 1990. Goa's Coastal and Overseas Trade from the Earliest Times till 1510 AD, *Goa Through the Ages*, New Delhi, Vol.II.

Gurav, R.N. 1969. *The Kadambas of Goa and their Inscriptions*, Unpublished Ph.D Thesis, Karnatak Univerisity, Dharwad.

Guzdar, Statira. 1980. *Quaternary Environment and Stone Age Cultures of the Konkan Coastal Maharashtra*, Bulletin of Deccan College & Post Graduate Research Institute, Pune.

Heras, H. 1928. Viragal of the times of Harihara II of Vijayanagara, *Quarterly Journal of Mythic Society,* Bangalore, pp.1-28.

—, 1932. Pre-Portuguese Remains in Portuguese India, *JBHS,* Vol.IV (3), pp.1-56.

—, 1980. A Newly Discovered Image of Buddha near Colva, Goa, *JBHS*, No.23, Bombay, pp.73-86.

Joshi, R.V. 1955. *Pleistocene Studies in the Malaprabha Region*, Karnatak University, Dharwad.

Joshi, R.V., & Bopardikar, B.B. 1972. Stone Age culture of Konkan (Coastal Maharashtra), *Archaeological Congress and Seminar Papers* (Nagpur), pp.47-57.

—,1991. Prehistoric Archaeology of Coastal India, *Indian Archaeological Heritage*, Vol.I, New Delhi, pp.91-99.

Kale, V.S., *et al* .1982. Late Quaternary Fossil Bone from Goa, *Current Science*, 52(2), pp.95-96.

—, 1982. Control of Dharwarian Strike on the Valley and Channel Forms of Dudhsagar River, Goa, *3rd IIG Conference*, Pune.

Kale, V.S., & Rajaguru, S.N. 1983. Some Aspects of the Quaternary History of Goa, *Bulletin of Deccan Post Graduate Research Institute,* Vol.XXXXII, Pune, pp.87-93.

—, 1985. Neogene and Quaternary Transgressional and Regressional History of the West Coast of India- An Overview, *Bulletin of Deccan college & Post Graduate Research Institute*, Vol.XLVI, Pune, pp.155-68.

Kamat, N.K. 1987. Gopakpattana through the Ages, *Goa through the Ages*, New Delhi, pp.251-269.

—, 1989. The Cultural Relation of Goa with Gujarat, *Essays in Goan History*, Concept Publishing Company, New Delhi, pp.1-16.

—, 1993. Stone Age Gallery, *Goa Today*, Panjim, pp.36-41.

Kashyap, P.C. 1984. *Surviving Harappan Civilization*, New Delhi.

Katti, M.N.1980. Arvalem Cave Inscription, *JESI*, Vol.VII, Mysore.

Krishnamacharlu, C.R., 1984. Siroda Plates of Devaraja, *Epigraphia Indica*, Vol.XXIV, pp.133-145.

Mahajan, Malti. 1989. *Cultural History of Maharashtra and Goa*, Sundeep Prakashan, New Delhi.

Mani, Vettam. 1975. *Puranic Encyclopedia*, Motilal Banarsidas Pvt. Ltd., New Delhi.

Marathe, A.R. 1981. *Geo-Archaeology of the Hiran Valley, Saurashtra, India*, Deccan College & Post Graduate Research Institute, Pune.

—, 1983. Prehistoric Exploration in the Mandvi and Zuari Basins of Goa, *Bulletin of Deccan College & Post Graduate Research Institute,* Vol.XXXXII, Pune, pp.104-107.

Mascarenhas, Antonio. 1987.*Goa from Prehistoric Times*, Vasco da Gama.

Mc Crindle, J.W.1987. *Ancient India as described in classical literature*, Eastern Book House, New Delhi

Merh, S.S. 1987. Quaternary Sea Level Changes- The Present Status vis-a-vis Records along the Coast of India, *Journal of Earth Sciences,* Vol.XIV (3), pp.235-50.

—, 1992. Quaternary Sea Level Changes along the Indian Coast, *Proceedings of Indian National Science Academy*, No.5 (58 A), pp.461-472.

Mirashi, V.V. 1977. Inscriptions of the Silaharas, *Corpus Inscriptionum Indicarum*, Vol.IV, Archaeological Survey of India, New Delhi.

Mitragotri, V.R. 1987. Vijayanagara and Post Vijayanagara Art and Architecture of Goa, *Goan Society through the Ages*, New Delhi, pp.270-82

—, 1988. Mahishasuramardini in Boat- A Rare Guleli Relief, *Purabhilekh-Purattatva*, Vol.VI(2), Panaji.

—, 1993. *A Socio-Cultural History of Goa from the Bhojas to the Vijayanagara,* Unpublished Ph.D. Thesis, Goa University.

Mitterwallner, G.V.1971. Die Hindu Kultskuptyurem Goas, *Band Gotlheien des Saivaitischen Kultkreises, Siva, Devi, Skanda*, Munich.

—, 1981. The Rock Cut Cave Temples at Arvalem, Goa, *Madhu-Recent Researches in Indian Archaeology and Art History*, New Delhi, pp.166-74.

Moreas, G.M.1931. *The Kadamba Kula*, New Delhi. (Reprint:1991)

Murthy, M.L.K., 1979. Recent Research on the Upper Palaeolithic Phase in India, *Journal of Field Archaeology*, Vol.6, pp.302-20.

Myers, B.S. & Coppleston, T. (Ed). 1993. *The History of Art*, Hamlyn Publication Group Ltd, London.

Nair, Vijayalakshmi & Selvakumar, R.A. 1979. The Ecology of Chaeograths in the Estuarine System of Goa, *Mahasagar-* Bulletin of the National Institute of Oceanography, pp.17-34.

Nambirajan, M. & Gaur, A.S. 1994. The Riverine Ports of Goa and Other Sites on the River Banks, *Proceedings of Fourth Indian Conference on Marine Archaeology of Indian Ocean Countries,* Vishakapatnam.

Narasimhaiah, B.1980. *Neolithic and Megalithic cultures of Tamil Nadu,* Sundeep Prakashan, New Delhi.

Neumayer, Erwin. 1983. *Prehistoric Indian Rock Paintings*, Oxford University Press, New Delhi.

Paddayya, K. 1982. *The Acheulian Culture of the Hunsgi Valley; A settlement perspective*, Bulletin Of Deccan College & Post Graduate Research Institute, Pune.

—,1985. The Acheulian occupational sites and associated fossil & fauna from the Hunsgi–Baichbal valleys. Penninsula India, *Anthropos 80*, pp.653-58.

—,1987. The Stone Age Cultural Systems of Baichal Valley,Gulbarga Dist, Karnataka; a preliminary report. *Bulletin of Deccan College & Post Graduate Research Institute*, Pune, 46; pp.77-100.

Pappu, R.S.1974. Pleistocene Studies in the Upper Krishna Basin, *Bulletin of Deccan College & Post Graduate Research Institute*, Pune.

Pedley, J.G., 1992. *Greek Art and Archaeology*, Villiers House, London.

Parameshwar, S. 1963. *Goa- An Evaluation of Historical, Political and Social History,* Unpublished Ph.D Thesis, Karnatak University, Dharwad.

Pitre, L.K., 1989. Buddhism in the History of Goa, *Goa Society through the Ages*, New Delhi, pp.16-24.

Poonacha, K.P. 1990. *Archaeology of Malnad Region*, Unpublished Ph.D Thesis, Karnatak University, Dharwad.

Quasim, S.Z., & Wafer, M.V.M. 1979. Occurrence of Living Corals at Several Places along the West Coast of India, *Mahasagar*-Bulletin of the National Institute of Oceanography, pp.53-58.

Rajguru, S.N. & S.J. Guzder. 1973. A Review of Research on Quaternary Sea Level Changes and Archaeological Sites in India, *Bulletin of Deccan Post Graduate Research Institute,* Vol.XXXIII, Pune, pp.193-208.

Rajendran, P. 1989. *The Prehistoric Culture and Environment*, New Delhi.

Ramesh, K.V. 1966-67. Four Stone Inscriptions from Goa, *Epigraphia Indica*, Vol.XXXVII, pp.282-88.

Rao, K.V. 1978. Stone Age Culture of Goa, *Archaeological Studies,* Vol.III, University of Mysore, pp.86-90.

Rao, Prabhakar & A.V. Raju. 1985. Geomorphology of Goa, *Earth Resources for Goa's Development* (Seminar Papers).

Rao, Seshagiri, R. 1985. *Flora of Goa, Diu, Daman, Dadar Nagar Haveli*, Vol.I, New Delhi.

Saha, B.C & J.M. Dasgupta.1992. *Birds of Goa*, Calcutta.

Sali, S.A. 1989. The Upper Palaeolithic and Mesolithic Culture of Maharashtra, *Bulletin of Deccan Post Graduate Research Institute,* Pune.

—, 1990. *Stone Age India*, Shankar Publishers, Aurangabad.

Satoskar, B.D. 1979. Gomantaka Prakrti ani Samskrti, *Subha Sarasvata* (in Marathi), Pune.

Sharma, M.J. 1982. *The Upper Palaeolithic Culture of India*, Agam Kala Prakashan, New Delhi.

Sharma, Y.D. 1956. Rock Cut Caves in Cochin, *Ancient India*, No.12, pp.93-98.

Shetty, B.V. 1984. *Studies in Karnataka history*, Sterling Publications, New Delhi.

Shirodkar, P.P. (Ed). 1984. Historic Saptakoteshwara Temple of Naroa, *Purabhilekh-Purattatva*, Vol.II(1), Goa, pp.108-17.

—, 1987. A Rare find of Mother Goddess at Kurdi, *Goan Society Through the Ages*, Goa, pp.9-15.

—, 1988. *Goa-Cultural Trends* (Seminar Papers), Directorate of Archives, Archaeology and Museums, Panaji.

—, 1990. Megalithic Culture of Goa, *Archaeology of Karnataka*, Directorate of Archaeology & Museums, Government of Karnataka, Mysore, pp 172-80.

—, 1994. Stone Age Bruisings and Rock Carvings of Goa- How old they Are?, Unpublished Seminar paper, Dept. of Archives, Archaeology and Museums, Government of Goa, Pananji.

Singbal, S. 1985. Environmental Study of the Waters of Mandovi-Zuari Estuarine Complex, Goa, *Earth Resources for Goa's Development* (Seminar Papers).

Sircar, D.C.1973.*The Saktha Pithas*, Motila Banarasidas, Delhi.

Sriram, K., & Prasad, K.N., 1979. Observations on the Geomorphology of Goa, *Journal of Geological Survey of India*, Bangalore, pp.608-14.

Srivastava, M.C.P., 1979. *Mother Goddess in Indian Art Archaeology and Literature*, Agam Kala Prakashan, New Delhi.

Soundarajan, K.V. 1981. *Cave Temples of the Deccan*, New Delhi.

Sundara, A., 1969. Some Aspects of Neolithic Sites in Malnad Region, *QJMS*, Vol.LIX.

—, 1972. Rock Paintings in Hire Benkal, *Unpublished Seminar papers, 59th Indian Society Congress*, Mysore.

—, 1974. Megaliths in the West Coast and Ghat Regions of Karnataka-A Study, *Journal of Karnataka University*, Vol.X, pp.62-71.

—, 1991. Prehistoric and Protohistoric Cultures of Dakshina Kannada, *Perspectives on Dakshina Kannada and Kodagu*, Dicennial Volume, Mangalore University, pp.41-63.

Varde, W.R. 1914. An Eye Copy of an Inscription in Devanagari Characters from Goa, *JBBRAS,* Vol.XXIII, P.107.

Wakankar, V.S. 1973. Bhimbetka Excavation, *Journal of Indian History*, No.51, pp.23-33.

Wanke, Lothar. 1977. *Zentralindische Felsbilder*, Graz, Austria.

Wheelar, R.E.M. 1947. Brahamagiri and Chandravalli in the Chitaldrug, Dist. Mysore State. *Ancient India no.4* pp.181-310

Original Sources

A.R.I.E – 1962-63

A.R.I.E – 1963-64

A.R.I.E – 1964-65

A.R.I.E – 1965-66

A.R.I.E – 1972-73

A.R.I.E – 1975-76

Harivamsa Purana – Venkateshwara Steam Press, Bombay.

Mahabharata – Geeta Press, Gorakhpur.

Skanda Purana – Geeta Press, Gorakhpur.

Ratnagiri District Gazetteer, 1880. Bombay.

INDEX

❑❑❑

Pl. 1 : View of the riverine section. Shigao.

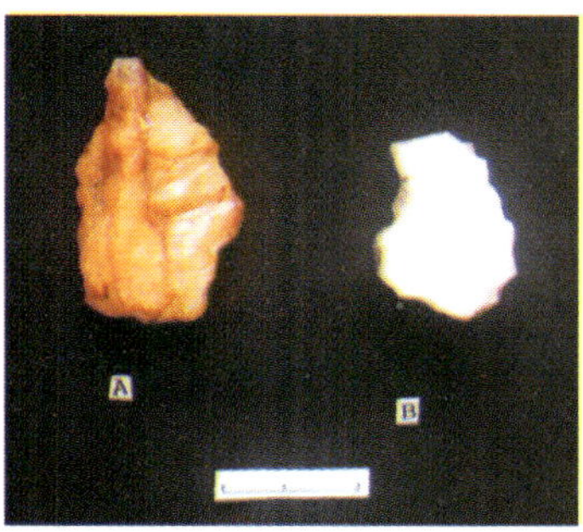

Pl. 2 : Middle Palaeolithic. Points.

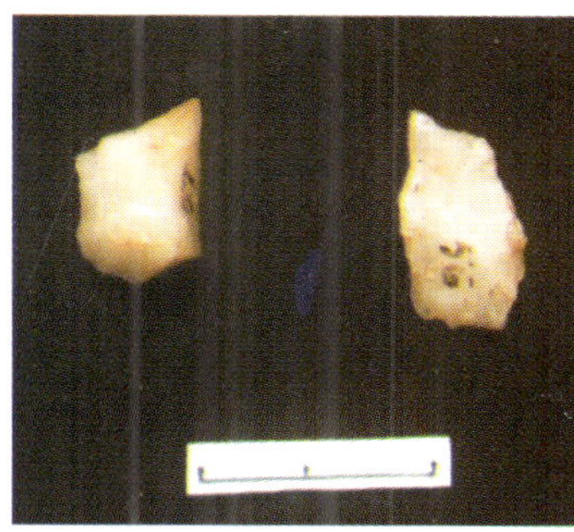

Pl. 3 : Middle Palaeolithic. Burins.

Pl. 4 : Middle Palaeolithic.

Pl. 5 : Molanguinim Cave entrance facing south.

Pl. 6 : Mesolithic. Flutted Cores and Flakes.

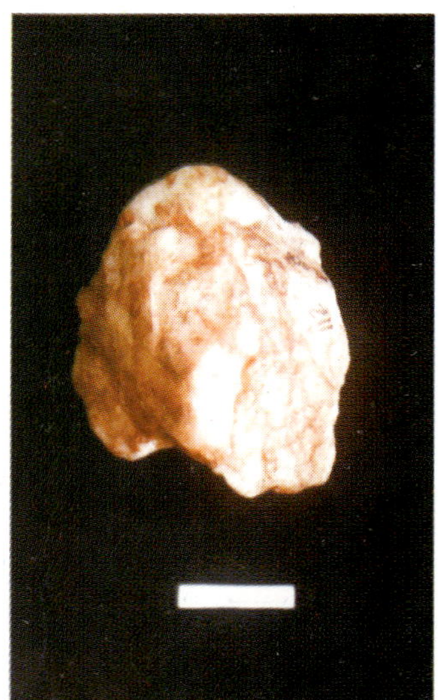

Pl. 7 : Mesolithic. Irregular Core.

Pl. 8 : Mesolithic. Cores.

Pl. 9 : Mesolithic. Flakes.

Pl. 10 : Mesolithic. Flakes.

Pl. 11 : Mesolithic. Bladish Flakes.

Pl. 12 : Mesolithic. Points.

Pl. 13 : Mesolithic. Points.

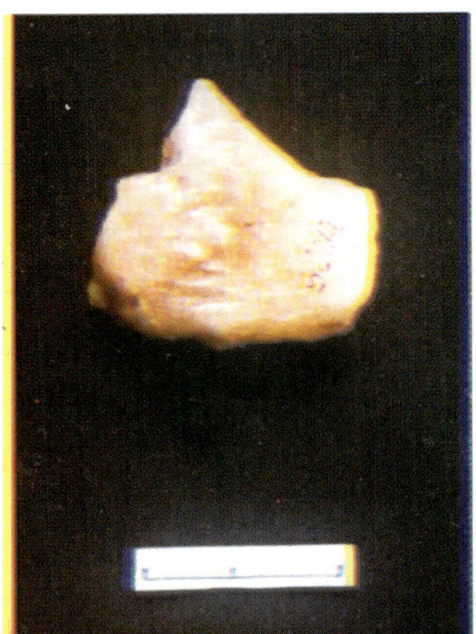

Pl. 14 : Mesolithic. Borer.

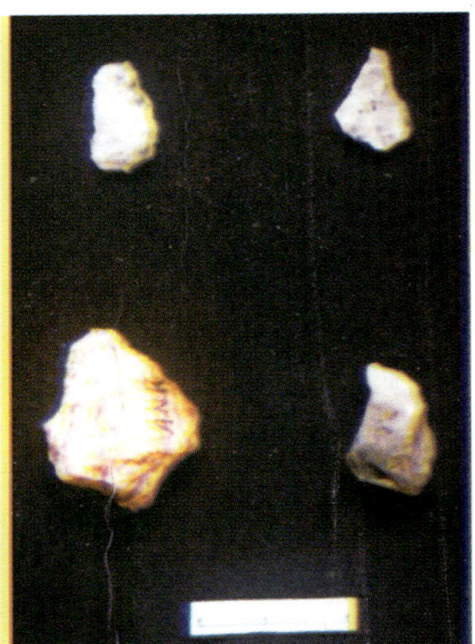

Pl. 15 : Mesolithic. Points and Lunates.

Pl. 16 : Underground Chamber. Chicalim.

Pl. 17 : Neolithic tools. Velha Goa Museum.

Pl. 18 : Stone Circle, Fatorpa.

Pl. 19 : Mother Goddess, Curdi.

Pl. 20 : General View. Usgalimol.

Pl. 21 : Chakravyuha. Usgalimol.

Pl. 22 : Bull. Usgalimol.

Pl. 23 : Agricultural Implement. (?). Usgalimol.

Pl. 24 : Dog (?) and trisul, Mauxi.

Pl. 25 : Engravings. Pansalimol.

Pl. 26 : Lion Sculpture, Shigao.